Death Is a Place

DEATH
IS A
PLACE

by

Beverly Ann White

VANTAGE PRESS
New York / Washington / Atlanta
Los Angeles / Chicago

FIRST EDITION

Copyright © 1986 by Beverly Ann White

Published by Vantage Press, Inc.
516 West 34th Street, New York, New York 10001

Manufactured in the United States of America
ISBN: 0-533-06918-1

Library of Congress Catalog No.: 85-91402

PREFACE

In this very private journal I have chronicled my own adventure in the valleys and the shadows of the place called Death, as I perceived it and as I experienced it. I know that no one learns from the experience of others; the pain that produces growth must be felt, not reported. However, my journal is also a family history that is now less private so that Edward and Daryn can know more intimately the lives and deaths of their aunts, so that Debra and Darcy can remember the details they had to remind me of, so that Pete can rejoin me in the splendor of our grief and growth, and so that I need never retell the tale of the deaths of my daughters, not even to myself.

I have told the story with cathartic honesty. If you are able to benefit in any way from reading this journal, I am grateful. If you laugh and cry, I have succeeded in some way. If you are a shade more comfortable with your own mortality and with the God who made you mortal, I am delighted.

Death Is a Place

CHAPTER ONE

The room was large and plain, like the hall of a church or a grange hall. Dani was standing in the middle of it, flooded with a radiant yellow light. She was glowing. She was wearing her wedding dress. I could hear a party going on around her; there were voices and music and the sounds of glasses clinking and dishes rattling. She was so beautiful there in that light as she turned and smiled at someone in another direction. Then huge hands reached down toward her, the palms cupped as one would hold one's hands to pick up a baby chicken. I spun around; my eyes followed the arms up to the face of Jesus, gently smiling and looking at Dani. I screamed at him, "What are you doing? Why are you taking her? Can't you see she is happy?" He didn't respond to me; he just continued to pick her up.

I awoke with a start and stared into the darkness. Since I often have dreams with a certain aura which indicates that what I have dreamed will later be relived in waking hours, I have made it a habit to tell someone of the content of those dreams. Then, later, when I yell, "I dreamed this!" I can add, "Remember? I told you about it." In the morning, I called my oldest daughter, Debra, who believes in my dreams and is receptive to acting as a witness to the fact that I did dream an event before it happened. I told her about the dream and then promptly forgot all about it. I didn't realize that this

1

dream was the first indication that we were approaching the boundaries of the place.

Friday was a good day but seemed to have a strange atmosphere about it, almost like a dream. I made Dani get up when Pete and Darcy did. Dani had been discharged from the navy in December and would be living with us until she married Roy in July. She had not yet gone to work so could have slept in, except that we had agreed to lose weight and get in shape for her wedding. She ran three miles every morning, while I biked along beside her, and then she mounted her bike for a nine-mile ride with me. We then showered and dressed and met Pete or Debra or sometimes Dani's next younger sister, Dawn, for lunch. Our routine was only slightly altered by the fact that Pete's parents, Ruie and Milford, were visiting us from Oregon. They were sleeping at Debra's apartment, about two miles away, and usually didn't get over to our house until it was about time to go to lunch. Today Dani was meeting Pete and Ruie and Mil for lunch. Deb was having lunch with Dawn and I was skipping lunch to get my hair done and have a manicure. I dropped Dani off at the restaurant and went on.

Roy, Dani's fiancé, would arrive at about 5 o'clock from San Diego. They had met while they were both in the navy in Florida. Dani had chosen not to reenlist but to take nurse's training as a civilian and then to reenter the navy when she had finished her four years of school. This decision would allow her more freedom in the future as she would not have to commit so many years of her life to the navy and would have more leeway when making career plans after nursing school. Roy, on the other hand, had decided to stay in the service and had stayed behind in Florida to attend a special school in sea and air rescue. Both Dani and Roy had been trained as helicopter mechanics and had flown out of Pensacola and Whiting Field as navigators and flight mechanics.

2

When Dani was discharged, I flew back to Florida and drove home with her in her little red Volkswagen. We had been home about two weeks before Roy called and asked her to fly back to Florida and drive across the country with him, as he would now be stationed in San Diego. Dani had arranged for him to be in California before she left her job as career counselor for their unit. They had arrived in California one week before this Friday. Roy spent the weekend with us and then went on to San Diego. Dani hadn't seen him for a week. They were both excited about the prospect of spending this weekend on our boat in Ventura. Ruie and Mil were to accompany us, as was Dawn.

Dawn graduated from Washington State University in June of 1983. Her father had been building a motel in Bakersfield, California, and had met an architect who wanted to hire a recent college graduate with a degree in architecture. Pete recommended Dawn. I edited and typed her letter of application and took her shopping for interview clothes. She drove down with her father and was hired, even before graduation. She moved down in June and was living in an apartment just a few blocks east of our rented condominium. She had a roommate, a boy who had graduated with her and had also found a job with an architectural firm in Bakersfield. They had developed a large circle of friends, did a lot of entertaining in their apartment, had joined a health club, and exercised twice a week. They never missed Monday night football at their favorite bar. Dawn and he had driven to San Francisco the weekend before and visited former schoolmates. Dawn had purchased a new outfit for the weekend and borrowed Dani's little red Volkswagen for the trip. This week, because her grandparents were visiting, Dawn had been over to visit us both Wednesday and Thursday nights. This was unusual; she dropped by occasionally but certainly not every night. She had hinted on Wednesday night that she wanted to go along

3

on the boat trip but I ignored her because I knew she hated crowded boats and we were certainly going to be crowded. Thursday morning she called her oldest sister, Debra, at the office where she worked for her dad and complained that even after hinting, no one had invited her along. Deb relayed the message to Pete, who got on the phone and laughingly told Dawn that hinting never worked with people as obtuse as we and that of course she could come along. We teased her Thursday night about almost missing the boat.

When I went to Florida to meet Dani for the drive home, I took along the afghan I was making for the boat. We were redecorating it in grays, removing all the orange, so the old afghan would have to be replaced. I crocheted my way across the United States. At night, we would spread out the squares on motel beds and decide on color combinations for new squares. When we got home, Dawn came over and helped us decide what squares should be located by which squares. Then Dani tucked all the yarn ends while I crocheted the squares together. By Thursday night, the afghan was done and dry-cleaned and waiting to be taken to the boat.

On Thursday, Dani and I went to the jeweler's store. Roy told her to go ahead and find the rings she wanted; they had agreed on a price range. He thought it would be much more efficient for her to go ahead and do the shopping; he was going to buy the ring she chose anyway. So we shopped. Dani bought Roy's wedding ring and his wedding gift, a gold pocket watch on a gold chain, at the first store we went to but she couldn't find the engagement and wedding rings that were meant for her. She got a little depressed. I encouraged her; I knew another store. We would shop there. We drove across town to a new shopping center with a modern, well-decorated jewelry store, staffed by a very pretty young woman who seemed to know her business well. And there was the ring. As Dawn would say, "It was calling her name."

4

(And then Dawn would hold her mouth very still and allow her lips to move only in one little corner as she piped, "Dani, Da-a-a-a-ani.") Dani was so excited; her eyes danced and her smile absolutely frolicked on her face. The woman gave Dani a booklet about diamonds which had a picture of that very ring on its cover. She would hold the rings for Roy to see that weekend. He would arrange the purchase then. Dani and I left the store and started home. As we drove, the energy seemed to drain away from Dani. Her body drooped and she looked depressed and sad. I commented on it; I said something about how tired she seemed and that she could take a nap when we got home. I wondered at the sudden drain of energy; I could feel it escaping from her body. That seemed a strange reaction to finding the one ring in the whole world that was calling one's name.

Rui and Mil, called Nana and Baba by their grandchildren, came over Thursday night. Dawn brought over a sample of the upholstery material we were going to use on the boat—almost as if she needed an excuse for coming over again on Thursday after being there on Wednesday. Dani and I were finishing the piecing of the quilt we had started when we arrived home from Florida. Dawn said she wanted to piece a quilt, too. She began selecting a pattern from a stack of old patterns that Ruie had brought along when she heard of our new interest in this ancient craft. Dawn chose the Star of Bethlehem pattern and made herself a template out of cardboard.

She was sitting on the raised hearth, a crackling fire behind her. As she sat there, she explained to her grandparents about the road to Ventura. "But," she said, "they have been working on it and there are plans to completely redo it. Of course, it won't be the same picturesque highway between orange groves and oleander, but it will be safer." I looked up from the quilt piece in my lap. Her eyes held me. I could not

5

look away. I was looking into antiquity. Aphrodite was staring at me. The Sphinx was coolly regarding me. I went past her face into those eyes. At last, I was able to look back down at my quilt piece. I had no idea how much time had passed. I was shaken.

Dani had seen the look. After Dawn mounted her little red Honda Aero, agreed that Dani and Roy would pick her up at her apartment at 5:30, and rode off, I asked Dani how she had interpreted that look. I offered the suggestion that maybe Dawn was trying to tell me that her adolescence was over and that we were adult friends now. Since she was twenty-four, that would be within the realm of possibility. Dani thought maybe so, and we dropped the subject. I didn't realize that I had been looking into the place.

We finished piecing that quilt Friday morning. We spread it out on the floor for Ruie to see. Dani gasped and said, "Oh, Mama, don't give me furniture for wedding presents. Make me quilts." We agreed that she would not start her quilt until Monday morning just in case I might need some of the pieces she would use along the border of this quilt. I started her quilt Monday morning.

I had my hair done at one shop on Stockdale Avenue, then had my nails done at another shop on the same street. Dawn's office was just a few blocks from the second shop. As I drove along Stockdale, headed to a clothing store, where I could do some furtive, solitary shopping, I passed Dawn's office. I heard a male voice.

I had heard that voice before. On August 1, while seated in my office in the mental health center in the Tri-Cities, I had heard that voice. It came from the corner behind me. It said, "If you want to be in Bakersfield in September, you will have to resign today." I turned and looked into the corner and replied, "You know, you are right." Of course, I didn't *want* to be in Bakersfield in September. I loved my job; I had, however, completed one phase of it and had not yet defined the next phase. It was a good time to join my family in California. I wrote a letter of resignation, called Pete and told him I was coming, and called a realtor and a mover. I sold the house in one week, with no haggling over the asking price. Pete and I were moved into the condominium in Bakersfield by September 1. While I was a bit hesitant to tell my co-workers in a mental health center and psychiatric hospital that the whole move had been instigated by a voice from the corner, I did mention it to one psychiatrist who didn't seem the least bit nonplussed by it. She only wanted to know what realtor had provided such fast service.

This time the voice said, "She's in there." I calmly replied, "I know it." I drove into the parking lot of the clothing store. I started to park. I didn't. I drove on. Without volition. I just drove on. I tried to park in front of another shop. I didn't. I drove on. I went home. Dani was there. I experienced joy that she was there. None of this surprised me. You see, we were within the boundaries of the place.

Dani was a good cook. She arranged food so nicely on a plate that the first person to be served was reluctant to disturb the design. Part of our regime during the last few weeks had been a fruit diet—as much as we wanted to eat as long as it was fruit. She arranged melons and oranges, bananas and grapes into delicate flowers, so intricate in design that we forgot they were edible and simply admired them as art. When Dani decided not to return to college after completing her freshman year, Pete and I informed her that we were not running an old age home for kids and that she had one week to find a job and an apartment. She found two jobs, because she was so unskilled that no one job paid enough to live on. She worked one shift at a Vips and then another shift at a Zips. She was a fry cook. She couldn't afford a car, so had to find locations that were close enough to her apartment to allow her to bicycle between home and jobs. Several months later, she was hired at a Thunderbird restaurant as a cook's assistant. There she learned to create beautiful salads and make sandwiches too pretty to eat. After a year there, she quit and went to work as a waitress for a while and then as a clerk in a delicatessen. She made enough money to buy a car, a used Volkswagen. Finally, in an act of independence and defiance, she walked into my house and announced that she had joined the navy. I deflated her swollen head and puffed chest by congratulating her on what I felt was a wise decision. She didn't tell the navy she could cook because she didn't want to be a military cook, but Dani could cook.

I sat in my favorite chair in the living room while Dani fussed in the kitchen. She was making egg salad and tuna salad to be used for sandwiches this weekend on the boat. She chopped and chopped and chopped. I called in to her that I would never be as good a cook as she was because I could never have the patience to chop and chop and chop like she did. She laughed and came out of the kitchen to show me the clear plastic bowls she had bought me. She didn't approve of the way I stored food in the refrigerator and had purchased this clear set so I would be able to see the contents, remember what I had stored, and use it. She was training me in proper food storage. As she talked and teased me, she kept fading out. I would be able to see her and hear her and then I could only sense the sunshine and the cool winter air and hear the bird song. And then she would fade back in. The energy levels of those in that place are different from ours. Those of us who are only visiting there can't receive sensory signals accurately and consistently from those who are of that place. I didn't question my strange sensory experience; I simply experienced my daughter fading in and out while she talked to me.

Dani looked darling. She had a new haircut. She had new

acrylic nails. She had firmed up and lost weight. She was wearing makeup, which she had to be reminded to do, but which enhanced her lovely eyes and long lashes. Her smile was infectious. Roy was coming; she was happy. She was wearing a gold sweater and pants outfit that I had given to her when I gained too much weight to wear it. It had an overlapping waistband that could be cinched down and she did have it cinched down. Roy and she were to go look at the wedding rings Dani had picked out. She had a friendship ring that Roy had given her on her right hand but that left hand was naked and all prepared in case Roy decided to buy the rings that afternoon. There was some question about when he would make the purchase because he did not have credit in California and had not had time to get a money order from back home in Michigan. Dani finished her task in the kitchen and I sat down with her at the kitchen table. We just chatted. We talked about the weekend on the boat, about the sleeping arrangements, about what time she and Roy would arrive, about how excited she was to be with Roy, and about Roy. Dani was an excellent story-teller and mimic. She was telling me of some incident in the navy, complete with accurate imitations of each actor. The room seemed to have a strange light, sort of yellow, and the air had a texture. It was a dreamlike setting. We talked. We smiled. We waited.

A shadow passed over the side of the refrigerator. Dani leaped to her feet and exulted, "Roy John!" She ran to the door and they embraced on the porch. I came into the entry hall as Roy was telling her how beautiful she looked. He thanked me for helping her stick to the beauty regime we had laid out. His pride in her showed in his face. Roy was a third-generation American of Finnish descent. He was blond, fair, not very tall, and, due to many long hours in a weight room, was very muscular. He was thin now because he had just completed that very strenuous air and sea rescue course, but his

9

muscles showed through his T-shirt. His teeth were a bit crooked. He looked as if he had just escaped from a Norman Rockwell painting. When he was bragging about Dani, and he often was, he would unconsciously point at her while he talked about her. He did this now. We stood there in the entry hall. I didn't ask him to sit down. I didn't offer him anything to drink. He had just driven five hours through Los Angeles traffic and I didn't do any of those things. It just didn't occur to me. I told Roy that I hoped he liked the ring Dani had chosen, that I was sure he would. He said that he was sure, too. I told them I would see them about 7:30 at the boat, that we would go ahead with Pete's parents, Ruie and Mil, and have the boat all cleaned up and ready for the weekend when they arrived with Dawn. They left. They walked around the side of the house to the parking lot in the back where Roy was to check on some fault in Dani's little red Volkswagen. Their voices seemed to fade in and out as they walked. Then I heard them walk back to the front of the house, talking all the time, to get in Roy's car and drive away. I didn't look at them. I never saw them again.

Ruie and Mil arrived with the cooler of bait they had brought from Oregon. Pete came home and we loaded the car. As we drove along I-5 toward Ventura, I read Nora Ephron's *Heartburn*. I laughed and read aloud the passage describing the supposed death of her mother and the nurse's shock at the sheet-draped corpse arising from the dead. I stopped reading when the language got a bit too strong for the tender Baptist sensibilities of my in-laws. I slept. Ruie and Mil were to sleep at a motel in order to ease the crowding on the boat. We stopped and checked them in and then all four of us went down to the marina. We scrubbed a week's accumulation of filth and salt from the boat. We stored all the food in the refrigerator. Milford got his tackle ready for the next day's fishing. Ruil and Mil and I walked along the harbor to a little seafood restaurant and ate dinner. We brought back fish sticks and French fries for Pete, who didn't want to leave his scrubbing. At about 7:30, he began to eat.

I kept watching the fence along the marina. I could envision the kids arriving and waving and waiting to be let in through the security gates. Then it was dusk and they still hadn't arrived. Pete left to take Ruie and Mil to the motel. We heard lots of sirens as we walked them up to the car. I stayed to let the kids in when they came. They didn't come. We finally made out their beds. Dani and Roy would sleep on the bridge. I put sleeping bags under for padding and a sleeping bag to sleep in and a comforter over that. We put up the bimini cover so the dew wouldn't soak them. Then I made up Dawn's bed in the front cabin. She was so skinny that I knew she would be cold. I made up one berth with several comforters. I patted the bed when I was finished because it looked so comfy and snuggly and I knew Dawn would be warm and comfortable there. Then Pete and I waited and watched the fence. We made out our bed in the salon. We crawled in. Pete fell asleep. I was still wearing my make-up and earrings because I was waiting for a horn to honk or someone to yell or a call on the marine radio to announce that the kids had arrived. I was angry. I told Pete when he stirred that those were the most inconsiderate kids I had ever seen and it must have been Dawn's fault. Dani and Roy were too conservative to ever deviate from our plans in such a manner. Dawn must have been showing off for her big sister and future brother-in-law; she probably had taken them far afield to some restaurant. Or maybe they were lost. But why not call us? How inconsiderate! I fell asleep sitting up with my arms crossed, grumping because I had raised such a bunch of ninnies.

Morning. I didn't remember hearing them come in. I checked. No one was in the beds we had made up. Pete demands that we use the bathrooms on shore whenever possible to avoid having to pump out the septic system on the boat. He left to go up to the bath house; I defied him and showered on the boat. As he left, I told him to check the parking lot. I was sure the kids were asleep in their car up there. I even told him what to tell those idiots for not waking us with a call on the marine radio. He came back to report that they weren't there. Now I was hurt. How could they do this to us? If they didn't want to come or if they were held up, why weren't they nice enough to let us know? Pete went to pick up his folks at the motel. I dressed and got ready to feed everyone breakfast. Ruie and Mil and Pete returned. We told them that the kids had not come down after all. Milford was upset because he could have slept on the boat if he had known they weren't coming. I called Debra to ask if the kids had left on time. I suspected she might be involved in whatever change of plans had taken place. She wasn't. She said they had left on time, as far as she knew. I called Dawn's roommate. He said they had left at 5:30. I had made these calls on marine radio, which can be monitored by anyone tuned in to that channel.

Pete now went up to use the land line phone by the bathhouse. What we were about to discover needed to be private. He called the state police. No, there hadn't been a wreck in Kern County, near home. Meanwhile, Debra was calling police departments from her house. She also got a "no" from local police departments. At about the same time, Pete and Debra both got the information that there had been a wreck in Ventura County but they didn't know if anyone was hurt. Where were we? They would call us back. Pete told them we were on our boat and gave them instructions as to how to reach us on marine radio. We waited. Ruie and I packed some handwork and books. We were expecting to spend the day in a hospital and wanted to have something to occupy us. I put on my makeup. No call came. Pete went back up to the phone by the bathhouse. Milford went up to do his morning constitutional in the rest rooms. I paced the floor, musing "How will this change our lives?" over and over again. I watched from the boat deck. I saw Pete walking back. He was stiff and gray. He climbed aboard the boat. I stood very still and stared at him.

"What is it?" I asked.

"They are dead," he said.

"All of them?" I whispered.

"They are gone," he said. "They are all gone."

Time did not exist. I was suspended in agony. I screamed. I fell to my knees. Pete grabbed me and tried to talk me into being silent. I stopped screaming long enough to explain to him that he must not try to stop me. He nodded. I resumed screaming and tried to climb over his body. Somehow my children were on the other side of him and I needed to get to them. He pulled his mother to her knees and he began to pray, "God, please welcome our children into heaven. Don't let them be afraid. Care for them. Make them welcome." As we prayed, Milford returned and climbed onto the boat. He saw us kneeling on the floor. I think I am the one that told him the kids were dead. He, too, fell to his knees, moaning as we prayed. That was the first and last sign he gave that he mourned them.

A call on the marine radio. It was Deb. She had been in contact with the coroner's office. She said, "Mama, they are . . ." I interrupted her. Somehow, just for a while, I wanted it to be private. I wanted to hold the knowledge that they were dead as I would hold them if only I could. "I know. Is Darcy there with you? Please just stay there together. Just stay there. Don't leave. We will be there as soon as we can." Darcy, our youngest daughter, was spending this weekend with her oldest sister. Deb told me that the coroner had cried and asked us to please not come there if we could avoid it.

They had had a terrible weekend and everything was in a turmoil. Dazed, we packed up Dani's tuna salad and egg salad. Milford walked along the dock and gave his bait to someone. The beds. What to do with the beds? Leave them and come back down later and stow everything? No. We would have to unmake our children's beds. We did. Somehow it seemed they had been there. I patted and caressed the sleeping bags, inside where their bodies would have been. I didn't take Dawn's bed apart. It, after all, was inside, where it could remain without getting damp or being stolen. I reached my hand inside, between the comforters, and rubbed where she would have slept. I glanced at the upholstery fabric laid out for her to decide whether or not it was the perfect choice for redecoration. I left it there.

We got in the car and drove. Back along the route where they had driven. Past the spot where they had left this place for that other place. We weren't certain exactly where the accident had happened. We watched for skid marks—there were thousands. That is a very dangerous stretch of highway. We watched for debris. There was none. I even looked for blood. We whimpered softly. I kept my hand on the back of Pete's neck. His parents sat in the backseat. They visited. They observed and commented on the passing scenery. They did not cry. They did not talk about the deaths. We drove on.

When we got to Debra's apartment, we hurried upstairs. I opened the door and looked at my two remaining children, my two blonde daughters. We have a family myth about the blondes. Blondes are scatterbrained, undisciplined, selfish, self-centered, very talented, great dancers and singers, but spacey—just plain spacey. Dani and Dawn were brunettes. They excelled in school, were neat and tidy with their personal possessions, were organized, paid their bills, respected other people's property, but were only spectators when it came to riding a horse or singing or dancing. Oh, Dani played the trumpet and Dawn played the piano but not very well. Dani could sing anything she had ever heard, including the lyrics to every commercial and the entire sound tracks of her favorite movies, but that was a function of memory, not musical ability. They would never be asked to perform, as Deb and Darcy often were. I looked at my youngest and oldest daughters and said, "My blondes. All I have left is my blondes." Was I intentionally cruel? I don't know. Debra was wounded. At sixteen, Darcy was too self-centered to even hear it or allow it to register. I hugged and held my daughters. Debra had been on the phone. She had what details were then known.

Just fifteen minutes from the boat, just at the turn before they would have left the dangerous highway and entered a safer stretch of four-lane road, just there they started into a curve. Coming from the other direction, coming from a village in Mexico, via immigration offices and farm labor camps, and most recently from a bar or park where he had had too much to drink, was a very small man who had no driver's license and no insurance. He drove off the road, into dirt, raised a cloud, and in that cloud of dust, he hit Roy and Dani and Dawn. He died instantly. Dani died instantly, too. Someone said she had been thrown out of the car. They were wrong; she had not. Dawn was not dead. She had been removed from the car and taken to a hospital—those sirens we had heard were announcing the arrival of our own daughter at the emergency room. She had never regained consciousness. Roy was not dead. He, too, was pried out of the car and taken to another emergency room. Roy and Dawn died within a few minutes of each other while in surgery.

Dani had a tattoo on the back of her shoulder. It wasn't even a pretty tattoo. It was a surrealistic butterfly; people had to ask what it was. She got it while doing a drunken sailor bit in Tennessee. When she came on leave that summer, we anchored the boat in the Snake River and spent many long

15

summer afternoons swimming and sun-bathing and diving off the top of the boat. Dani never took her T-shirt off. She would look at me intensely, defying me to notice that something was wrong. I noticed the look, but didn't rise to the bait. When I finally did spot the thing, my only comment was that it wasn't a very pretty butterfly. Dani had an appointment with a plastic surgeon next week. She was going to have that silly thing removed because it would show through the back of her wedding dress. When the coroner asked us to assist them in differentiating between the two bodies, we forgot to mention the butterfly or the acrylic nails. We told her that Dani was shorter; that's all we could think of.

Now. What does one do? There must be things to do. What? Call. Call Roy's parents. But what is their number? Where do they live? The name of the town came to me: Ironwood. There were many listings with that last name in that town. I couldn't get them. Ruie said to call our family and tell them. Not yet. No, it is still ours. Just ours. The coroner said we must have a mortuary come get the bodies. A mortuary? We moved to this town in September; today was February 25. What mortuary? We called Dawn's boss. He had lived in this town all of his life. He recommended a mortuary. We called them. They would have to bring us forms to sign allowing them to pick up the bodies. They wouldn't be able to go down to Ventura to get them until tomorrow. We needed to go home. We packed up our grandson, Debra's son, Edward Arthur White II, and our daughters and went home.

Pete and I went into our room to change clothes. I looked at my silent husband, the man who after twenty-eight years of marriage was just learning to say what he felt and thought. I was suddenly struck with the realization of what these deaths could do to a man who was just coming out of his shell. I went to him, put my arms around his shoulders and said, "Please don't lock yourself away from me. We must

16

stay open with each other. If we do not, we could lose each other, too. This could destroy our entire family unless we carefully remember to stay open with each other." He agreed and he lived up to that agreement in the months that followed.

Now the calls. First I called Pete's little sister, Becky. She had been especially close to the girls and to us. I told her, "Becky, I have bad news. Dani and Dawn are dead." She screamed and screamed and screamed. Her husband grabbed the phone. He is a policeman and more adept at handling such traumatic information. I asked him to notify all family members in that city. He said he would and would then start almost immediately for Bakersfield for the funeral. Then I called my brother. He hadn't really known the girls, but I had a job for him, too. He was to call all of my family and let them know. And he was to do it in such a way that they understood that they were not invited to the funeral. My parents and sister did not know my daughters at all. My mother had attended Ruie and Mil's fiftieth wedding anniversary celebration in December and had remarked to Dani that "I could have passed you on the street and not known you." That had wounded Dani. My children never understood the selfishness that made my parents unable to love and share. My children had not visited my parents' home since infancy; they had never been invited. My parents did not attend Debra's wedding or Dawn's college graduation or any other family celebrations. I spent many quiet times with my children, explaining to them that it was no lack in them that made their grandparents ignore them. As I spoke to my brother, I remembered these facts with a cool anger. I told him that grandparents who do not come to our weddings do not come to our funerals. I did not have the energy to cope with their guilt—or, God forbid, their lack of it—at my daughters' funeral.

Next, I called my best friend, Mary Lou. I told her what had happened, much as she had told me several years before

17

of her son's death by drowning. She asked what she could do and I said, "Come." They got in their car and drove for sixteen hours, straight through from Prineville, Oregon, to Bakersfield, California. Mary Lou had known and loved my girls. She had lived next door to me when I was five years old, and our friendship had never wavered across those years. We had traveled to Europe together, and shared birthday celebrations, small trips, vacations, and boat trips down the Columbia River. Mary Lou had often visited and enjoyed our family. Also, she had been through this whole process and would know what she now regretted and what she was glad she had done the way she did. I needed to know those things.

The phone started to ring. And Pete and I began the learning process that was our daughters' death, and funerals.. What we learned and how we learned it is so important that I must tell you how it came about and what it was.

CHAPTER TWO

The phone rang. It was Nancy, Dawn's boss's wife. She quietly told me that she had lost a daughter in a car accident. Could she come over? They came. Mostly they listened to Pete and me talk. We sat in the living room, but it seemed cold and too large. Nancy said that there was nothing she could tell us except that we would have to experience this ourselves, that each person had a different experience. She didn't say it, but now I know that it is like birth. Each mother knows that her birth experience is unique. There are, however, some things that can be universally experienced if one will allow oneself to do so. If at birth one allows doctors and nurses to become drug pushers, the joy is obliterated behind the dope. Much of the pain remains, but the joy is gone. Intuitively knowing this fact, I refused offers of sleeping pills and Valium. I felt around in my body and replied that my body seemed to be handling it. No thanks. After a while, Nancy and her husband, Don, left, promising to return later with food.

Back to the phone. I must call the girls' friends. First Mike. Dawn and Mike had spent the last five years in the same architecture classes and developed a friendship that had been rewarding and entertaining. Mike's mother answered the phone and I told her first, thinking that she would tell Mike. Instead, she brought him to the phone. Again, I assigned the duty of relaying the news to that certain circle of friends and acquaintances. Mike said, "I feel like I ought to come." My heart leaped at that need to come and share with us. I thanked him and asked him to sing at the funeral. That was the first planning; it had begun to evolve almost on its own.

Now to contact Dani's friends. I called Theresa in Florida. Dani and Theresa were in the same aerobics class; Theresa taught it and Dani substituted for her sometimes. Theresa's husband was a navy chief who had been serving in the same unit as Dani and Roy. Theresa was to have been Dani's bridesmaid in July. She let me tell her and then told me that the navy had already called the base and everyone there knew. Dani and Dawn had had no current California identification with them when they died. Dani had just arrived in the state from Florida, and Dawn had not gotten around to getting a new driver's license in the eight months since she had moved. Roy, however, had had current navy identification; the coroner had notified the navy immediately, and San Diego had called Florida. An officer had been dispatched to Roy's home in Michigan; his mother knew long before we did, even though we were waiting just fifteen minutes away. Theresa couldn't come to the funeral. None of Dani's navy buddies could come, but they were planning a memorial service on the base. They would record it and send us the tape.

The family huddled in the tiny little den. Occasionally someone would drift out to the living room, but its seeming vastness and coldness would send them back to the floor in the den. There was only one large leather chair and a desk chair in that book-lined room, so we sat on the floor.

Roy's sister called. Dani and Roy stopped at her home in Colorado on their trip across the States from Florida to California. Although Dani had gone home with Roy the summer before and met all of his family, his sister Bonnie hadn't been at her parents' home so they had not met. Dani told me in her storyteller fashion every detail of the visit to Bonnie's. They had skied; Bonnie and her husband were ski instructors

20

and had loaned Dani and Roy clothes and equipment. Inadvertently, Dani had been sent down a double-diamond slope. Dani was often caught making herself sound a little better at a skill than she was, and this time Bonnie was convinced that Dani was an expert skier. Actually, she had skied only one season in her life. Dani did the slope on her bottom, scooting down the steep incline. Near the bottom, she went into a grove of trees and put her skis back on and skied out, pretending that she had schussed the whole hill. She no sooner completed her fake finish than Roy arrived, all white-faced and worried. He knew she couldn't ski very well, discovered the mix-up, and sped down the hill, expecting to find her crumpled body around every curve. He was delighted with her for having transversed the hill, even though it had been on her bottom. They posed together for photographs, pointing at the double diamond on the trail marker. Bonnie was delighted with Dani and with Roy for having produced such a congenial future sister-in-law.

Bonnie knew that Dani was dead—the navy had told her mother—but she didn't know that Dawn died, too. In a whispery little voice, she said, "Oh, no! You lost two daughters. Oh, no. My mother will just die." Her mother had been trying to reach us; Bonnie had succeeded first. I got the number from Bonnie and called her mother, Gloria. I told her everything I knew about the accident, how Roy looked the last time I saw him, and exactly what he said and did the last weekend he spent with us. She hadn't seen him since August, when he had brought Dani home to meet the folks. She had loved Dani, but had not had her favorite son to herself because of Dani's presence. Roy was a good son and called home and wrote and sent cards often. I told Gloria that I found the flag up on the mailbox when we got back to the house from the beach. Since no one had been home to mail anything, I checked to see what was in there. Roy had sent his little sister

21

a birthday card. We talked about how nice it was that, in the midst of looking at wedding rings and being with Dani after a week's separation, Roy had taken time to buy and mail a card to his little sister. Gloria and I promised to talk often as we planned funerals and learned to mourn.

Roy's body had been claimed by the navy. His father wanted it cremated; Gloria did not. She had not seen her son since August; she wanted his body. His father overruled her objections, and Roy was cremated, wearing his dress blues. Our children's bodies had not arrived from Ventura. We waited, huddled in the den.

Dawn's roommate skidded his car to a stop in front of our apartment. I ran out. He was putty-colored and in shock. I had made several attempts to reach him by phone but he had left the apartment early and gone to the office. I thought he was playing golf and had given up. The people who worked with Dawn had tracked him down and told him that Dawn had been killed. He said that he had suspected something was wrong when I called him that morning, but he had gone to the office without pursuing it. I led him into the den. He sat in the leather chair and I sat on the footstool. As I told him what we knew about the accident, I kept patting him and holding his hand. As I talked, I saw Dawn walk into the room. She cocked her head and looked at me from under her brows, as if checking on my behavior. She sat down on the footstool beside me and watched me, never smiling, for a little while. She was wearing an outfit I had never seen; it was the skirt and blouse and jacket that I would later iron and take to the funeral home for her to wear in her casket. Somehow, inside, there is a way that we can talk to the dead. There is a voice, but it makes no audible sound. I told her in that voice that I would take care of him. She nodded and left. I was not surprised. I did pat the stool where she had been sitting but I did not comment to anyone that she had been there. We were in the place and the rules are different there. I don't remember when the roommate left.

Night came. We weren't eating. The time of day really didn't matter. It was simply night and therefore time to go to bed. We slept. It was an escape from the reality of that day. Morning was difficult. We woke; we wept. It was still true. The girls were dead. This was helplessness. We are people who do things about things, but there was nothing to do. Dorothy Parker would have appreciated the tears in our ears. Finally, Pete (his real name is Edward Arther, but he has come to be called Pete) said that we might as well get up, that it was sort of silly to just lie there and cry. We dressed in dark suits. Somehow there was a need to be severely and seriously attired.

Sunday. A day to plan a funeral. People were calling. People, some of them strangers, came to the house. One must. Until this day, I had never known what was needed of me when a friend began to walk in this valley. Now I knew. One must call and talk to the bereaved person. One must not settle for talking to the friend delegated to answering the phone. It helps so much to tell the story to people, over and over. I learned how important it is to go to the house, to take food, to look around and see what needs doing and do it. If that doesn't seem appropriate, then one must just sit and visit. Those who are far away should call and then send flowers and a card or letter, saying how much they sympathize. When the cards started coming, each trip to the mailbox was an adventure. People reached out and touched with those cards, people we hadn't seen or heard from in years. And many people who should have didn't. The mourners are very aware of who does and who does not.

Mark Russell was a co-worker of Dawn's. They weren't especially good friends but he spent his days with her just a few desks away. He brought his wife and baby boy and some

23

food and paid a call. We had never seen Mark or his wife before, but the call was appreciated. They sat around and visited and talked about Dawn and the funeral. We played with the baby. Then they left. Jerry Todd is a business associate whose firm does business with my husband's firm. Pete and he are friendly, but Pete and I had never met his wife and I didn't know either of them. He dropped by. He just opened his arms and hugged me. It seemed perfectly normal to be hugging this nice stranger in my doorway. After the hugging, he explained who he was. His wife would be by later. He left.

My best friend, Mary Lou, and her husband, Gordon, arrived in the afternoon, having driven all the way from Oregon. We were still huddled in the den. It seemed that we had to stay there until Dani and Dawn's bodies were transported to the mortuary, then we would be free to move around. But for now we must sit in a small space and wait. At about 5 o'clock, the mortuary called; the bodies were there. We could come out and make the arrangements now. Mary Lou and Gordon went with us.

Debra and Darcy and Pete and I, all that was left of our family, went to the mortuary. I think we were hostile at first. The director was a young man who was very patient with our initial hostility. He smiled; he acted more like a mental health counselor than a funeral director. We explained that we had some strong ideas about how a funeral should be and that we would not be discouraged. He was agreeable. He thought that each funeral should be unique; he told us about some exceptional ones that he had helped with, such as that of the old lady who collected rag dolls. The funeral parlor had been stuffed with Raggedy Anns and Andys. He talked about the parents of a dead infant, who released a helium-filled heart-shaped balloon as they left the chapel to indicate to God and their friends that they were willingly letting that child return

24

to God. We relaxed. This funeral would be a unique celebration of the lives of our daughters.

Now the business: would they be embalmed? No. Their bodies would be allowed to decompose naturally. But if they were not embalmed, we asked, could their bodies be cleaned up? Not very well. They would bleed fluids. A compromise: they would be washed as well as they could be and then wrapped in a plastic bag before being dressed. That way, the casket and their clothes would not be soiled. The caskets. Were we ready to look at caskets? Once again the director, Jim, began to act like a mental health counselor; he watched us closely and we watched him watching us. Mary Lou and Gordon hung back; they, too, were concerned that this might be a very emotional time. It was not. Pete and I and Debra and Darcy shopped for caskets. We wanted something close to a pine box, but not quite a pine box. Pete found them. They were made of oak and cherry. The oak one was for Dawn because her drafting table was oak and the ornamental wood of the racquet club she had helped us design and build was oak. Her life in the last two years had been very much involved with oak. Dani's was cherry. Dani had liked traditional furniture and had a desk made of cherry. The wood caught the light and reflected it warmly into the room. We inspected the interiors. It was important to me that they not have their heads propped up on pillows. Pillows are for sleeping people; our daughters were not sleeping. They were dead and they would act like it, thank you. Fine. No pillows.

We chose a viewing room. I was not familiar with this part of funerals. Now I understand why my friend Emily was insulted and offended when I didn't go to the viewing room when her husband died. I just didn't know anything about that custom. Now we learned. There were several beautifully decorated rooms in which the coffins would rest until the funeral. Flowers would be displayed there and there was a guest book for those who had come to pay their respects—and that is what they were doing—to sign. We giggled as we chose. Dawn had wonderful taste in interior design; I could sense her dismay when I opened the door to the room done all in red velvet. I heard her say, "It looks like Early Bordello." Finally we found one big enough for two caskets and done in a very tasteful manner with antique furnishings. A lovely old secretary held the guest book. I knew that either Dani or Dawn would have loved to possess that old desk.

Now the graves. We rode out through the cemetery. No, not near the mausoleum. Too artificial. No, not near the lake or the rose garden. What about over there on the hill? We walked down the hillside from the road on top. We could see the whole valley and the Tehachapi Mountains. It was quiet and there was a soft breeze. The sky was winter blue above us. Yes, this was the place. We found Row 2013, for Pete's lucky number 13, and then graves 2 and 3, because Dani and Dawn were our second and third daughters. Jim wasn't too thrilled with that selection because that left 1 and 4 unsold and single. Too bad. It would be graves 2 and 3.

Back to the office of the mortuary. We had to order gravestones. Small. Dogwood trim on Dani's because she had lived on Dogwood Lane in Florida and was a dogwood kind of girl. Dawn's would have columns because she had drawn so many of them in her art classes and architecture studies. It felt so good to find little things that celebrated their lives. The headstones would be carved with just their names: Dani Lynn White and Dawn Marie White, and their dates: 1958 to 1984 and 1959 to 1984. No. Debra and Darcy and Pete disagreed; they felt that the stones should say something more. So we began to try to find a simple phrase that would indicate how we felt about Dani and Dawn, both alive and dead. At last we discovered the phrase waiting for us: "With Love."

Jim turned into a mental health counselor again. It was

time to go through the girls' effects and to go where their bodies were. Mary Lou and Gordon, possibly remembering their own drowned son, again began to hang back. I was not afraid. I knew my family wanted to be where the girls were. We were ready. Jim lectured us. They had been badly traumatized by the accident. Dawn had been given oxygen, which had discolored her face. If we were to actually look at them we would never be able to remember them any other way. He made us promise not to look. Pete helped him elicit that promise from me. Pete was frightened; he was their father, not their mother. Their bodies were part of my body. I wanted to look, but Jim and Pete made me promise not to. I didn't, but I touched.

They lay side by side on gurneys in an ugly storage room in the basement. A thin white sheet draped each body. I could see every detail of their bodies. I immediately walked to their hands. First I felt the shape of Dani's right hand. I wanted so much to just lift the sheet and see her hand, but I was afraid that her pretty nails were broken and I guess I didn't want to see them that way. Maybe I wasn't as brave as I thought I was. I just caressed her hands through the sheet. I felt her head. I could feel hair but I could not distinguish the shape of a human head. It was huge and almost square. Running my hand along her shoulder, I crossed to the next gurney and touched Dawn's head. It felt head-shaped. Now down her side to her left hand. Ah, her old bony hand. She had never had pretty hands. The nails were spatulate and every knuckle stood out like she had cracked them all her life, which she had not. No daughter of mine cracks her knuckles. I loved Dawn's bony hands. Then I ran my hands down her legs, caressed her big, old size-10 feet. Never had a really pretty pair of shoes that was comfortable enough to do more than hobble in. They just didn't seem to make shoes to fit those feet. Now along the bottom of the gurneys to Dani's feet,

27

her little feet, the smallest feet in the family. She had pretty feet but now they were turned down hard. From my old physiology classes, the word *brain-dead* flashed through my head. Dani had died of a broken neck. Her brain had died before her body did. Now everyone approached those two sheet-draped forms and began to caress and fondle them—Deb first, then Darcy. Mary Lou touched them and seemed bemused. Now Pete felt their forms with the palms of his hands. It was a time to love them. We didn't weep; we loved.

Jim brought in their effects. Dawn had worn no jewelry. Could it have been stolen? No, she probably wouldn't have worn any jewelry to the beach. A woman handed me Dani's friendship ring that Roy had given her. She had been so proud of that ring; it had really been a pre-engagement ring and represented the fulfillment of her dream of marriage and living happily ever after. She never really was convinced that in all likelihood she would not live happily ever after. I reacted violently. I almost attacked the poor woman holding the ring out to me. "That was Dani's ring," I said. "Put it right back on her hand right now." I didn't want to think about how badly that ring was bent. We then believed that Dani had been thrown out of the car. I hated the image of her hand hitting the pavement and bending that ring.

Their overnight cases were there and their purses. Dani had carried my navy blue purse at my insistence. Dani always liked little things; we often called her Dainty, instead of Dani. She would carry a miniature white purse in every season and with every outfit. Friday morning I saw that white purse coming out of the closet and set my foot down. "You will carry my navy blue purse to go with your navy blue shoes. That white purse is out of season and too small for that outfit anyway." Reluctantly, she transferred her possessions from the white one to the blue one. Now that blue purse was torn and asphalt was imbedded in the side of it and there was dried

28

blood on it. I kept running my palm over that dried blood, my daughter's blood. There were bits of gravel stuck in the torn leather and dark blood. In a soundless void of palpable white light, I touched my daughter's blood, while my breath stopped and my heart rested. I was in the place again.

The satchels contained the girls' weekend clothes, make-up, toiletries, and their cameras. Both cameras had partially exposed rolls of film in them. These had to be developed quickly. We had to have one more glimpse of our daughters and their lives and the objects they had photographed. The clothes were now leftovers; the make-up was garbage, a waste product; the deodorant; the perfume; the funny little turquoise compact with no mirror and no powder; what does one do with these things? The girls had touched them; they had been intimate with these fluids and bottles. They can't be thrown away, not yet. And the identification cards. Dawn was so proud of her very own American Express card and her VISA. She would carefully budget some purchase, pay for it with her card, and then immediately send in the money. She firmly believed this was her duty, that she was establishing good credit. And her business card. She had distributed that so proudly. And the photographs in their wallets of friends; their little nephew, Edward Arthur II; their parents; themselves. We carried these things home with us.

Two little booklets were in Dani's purse: *All about Diamonds*, with the photo of her engagement ring on the cover, and *Together for Life*, with a picture of a bride and groom running through a meadow on its cover. The priest had given it to her the week before. She and Roy were to study it this weekend and design their wedding ceremony by selecting the readings from it. And the woman handed me a brown manila envelope, labeled

292-84
293-84

29

I don't know if Roy was 291-84 or 294-84. I thought about the other two hundred and ninety people who had died in 1984 in Ventura County. I looked at the title of the booklet. Together for life, together in death. I hoped they had been snoozing or laughing. I hoped Dani's head had been turned back toward Dawn and that one of them had been telling a story at which the other two were laughing. The directions from the highway to the boat moorage were also tucked in that purse. They almost made it to the spot where they would have needed them.

We left. We turned back and looked for the last time at the sheet-draped forms of our daughters. We would never see them again. And I regret that. I should have prepared my daughters' bodies for burial. I stood there and told Jim that, in another time, I would have washed them and dressed them myself. He replied that the parents of dead infants were still encouraged to do that, but not when the bodies were so mutilated. I let myself be persuaded, but I will always wish I had stood my ground. In some way, those bodies were my body. My daughters were left to strangers in the end. I hope they forgive me.

We were drained. We drove home. People had been coming and leaving food and offers of help. One should not do that. One should not say, "If you need anything, just call me." Mourners never do. It is not the mourner's responsibility to figure out what is needed. If there is anything one can do, one must simply do it. One must not ask, but one should offer one's skills or talents. Joan Todd, the wife of the fellow who hugged me at the front door, left word that she would sing at the funeral if we needed her. We thanked her and told her we had someone. We went to Dawn's apartment and chose the outfit she had worn to San Francisco and to the den when she checked on me for her to be buried in. I didn't choose underwear. Somehow I couldn't bear to think of them being buried naked in those plastic bags, but I also couldn't tolerate the idea of forcing mutilated breasts into bras. And I didn't take shoes. Their feet would be naked. Dawn had washed the outfit out by hand but she hadn't ironed it. I ironed her clothes for the very last time. Dani would be buried in her wedding dress. I did not want that lovely tiara placed on that battered head; she would hold it in her left hand with the veil down over her legs. People came. They hugged. One must always hug the people walking in the shadows of this place.

We had to tape the music that would play in the chapel during the service. Debra brought over records that she knew to be Dawn's favorites. She and Dawn had shared their love for music and both had extensive tape collections. I chose several selections from the two records Deb thought Dawn would have chosen, among them Shadowfax's "Flight of Angels." Mary Lou and I lay on Darcy's bed, wrapped in comforters, while Mark, an ex-boyfriend of Deb's who had dated both Deb and Dawn and who was a sound man for a radio station, did the taping. He just needed to be involved and near. I realized as he sat there that these young friends of my children would need help facing the deaths of their peers. Helping them would help me. I was grateful for that realization. Mary Lou and Gordon left to go to their motel. People would be arriving all day tomorrow; it would be a big day. We undressed and went to bed. We slept peacefully and soundly, holding each other.

Monday, the day before the funeral. My aunt Lois and my brother John would be arriving by plane. Pete had just built a motel; the owner called to say that it would be closed to the public, if need be, in order to house our guests. Wonderful! All our guests would sleep there. Rich and Kathy arrived. Rich is president of a bank my husband founded and was to act as master of ceremonies at the funeral. Dawn's friends began to arrive. These young people had just graduated from college and started low-paying internships with architectural firms. Older brothers and sisters and some parents had paid for traveling expenses so that they could come here from all over the West Coast to say good-bye to their friend. As they arrived, there was hugging and I found myself patting them on the back and assuring them, "It's all right. It's all right." It was comforting to have them here. They are a part of Dawn; they loved her, too.

The funeral was beginning to take shape. As we sat and visited and told stories about Dani and Dawn, it occurred to me that each story was a little piece of the girls that no one else could hold unless it was shared. I began to ask each person who told a story if he or she would please tell that story tomorrow at the funeral. We assured everyone that if they cried, they could stop and sit down, but that we would be so grateful for their attempt at telling the story for everyone. I could see them consider and then agree.

We needed a minister. We are members of an organization that combines Yoga and Christianity and has few ministers, even fewer who are free to travel to Bakersfield to perform a funeral. And, then, how would my Baptist family react to an ocher-robed yogi? No. We would need something more traditional for the folks. Nancy, Dawn's boss's wife, suggested her pastor, a Unitarian minister. She reminded me that Unitarians have nothing to sell and will happily perform whatever kind of service we would be comfortable with. We called the Rev. Clifton Gordon; he was in our living room in just a few hours. His first words were, "I am not familiar with the organization you worship with, but if you will tell me what kind of service they would perform, I will do my best to replicate it." His gentle face, his quiet manner, and his smiling but sympathetic demeanor were a gift from God. No need for hostility here. We told him that we would have Rich introduce himself and ask people to share their experiences with the girls. After people had talked as much as they would, Darcy would sing "May I Have This Dance for the Rest of My Life?," a song she had been practicing to sing at the wedding reception for Dani and Roy. Then Mike would sing "The Shadow of Your Smile." Then we would like him to read some poetry and Scripture; I would trust his judgment as to what he would read. Then Dawn's friends and their policeman uncle, Becky's husband, Ken, would carry first Dani and then Dawn to the cars. The mourners were to be instructed that we would walk across the cemetery to the grave site and that the caskets would be lowered into the graves before we left. If anyone would rather not watch that, they were free to say good-bye to Dani and Dawn and leave. The Reverend Gordon left with promises to arrive at the house at 10 o'clock the next morning to ride with us to the mortuary. Now we had to take the clothes to the mortuary.

Debra went to work today. She cannot deal with her grief and pain. She carries an especially heavy load. Deb never adjusted to being one of a crowd; she wanted to be an only child and always resented the fact that she wasn't. As a child, she heard a different drummer than did Dani and Dawn. They were very close, and Debra was alone at the top. For the last year, Dawn had been in Bakersfield with Deb and Dani was far away in Florida. Deb and Dawn had become friends; then Dani came home. Deb reacted as a jealous sibling and worked very hard to keep Dani and Dawn from reestablishing the friendship of their childhood and early teens. Her efforts culminated in a yelling match on the phone just the day before the two girls she wanted to keep apart died together. Debra called me to say that Dawn had said something snide about Dani and that Dawn felt that I favored Dani. I responded with, "Why are you doing this, Debra? This is not kind; this is not loving; this is not good. I will talk to Dawn on the boat this weekend and we will get it settled. You just stay out of it and let each of us work out our own relationships." I also told her that Dani was very hurt by her behavior. Then I hung up on her. Dani was in the room and overheard my end of the exchange. Her face immediately took on an expression she had worn since early childhood at times like these: she looked as if she were saying, "I am a bit disgusted that the world is this way. I am not mad at anyone in particular, but this is not the way I would like the world to work." I told Dani that she would have to work out her relationship with her sisters, that it was only a matter of time before the adjustment to her reentry into the family would be over, that I knew she was capable of courting both of her sisters, and that this recent outburst was an indication of her imminent success. Thursday night, Dani worked at courting Dawn by dropping the self-conscious silliness she had been portraying; she was her old friendly self. Dawn responded warmly. They were going to be all right.

But Deb now retreated into her work. The office was kept open; the job, a 260 unit motel under construction, was humming. Joe, our foreman, who had been to Vietnam and tangled with some Agent Orange and was consequently unable to deal with frustration and emotion, could not deal with the deaths directly so ran the job as he felt Pete would, as his contribution to the family.

So Pete and I rode alone together to take the clothes to the mortuary. As we turned into the driveway, it struck me how much like birth this was: we took a layette to the hospital when the girls were born and we were taking another layette now. Their births had changed the number in our family; their deaths once again altered the head count. There was pain and joy in the birth process; there was also pain and joy in their deaths. And there was inescapable growth for the parents in both instances. We also took the taped music for the service the next day and the obituary I had typed out for each of them. We chose the type style and color of paper for the funeral cards. Many people who would be attending had never met our daughters; they worked with Pete or were people in the community who were responding to our loss and our recent move and were attending in order to give support. I had no idea how many people would be so generous and thoughtful as to attend a funeral just so the parents of the dead ones would be surrounded and supported. God must have a special place in His heart for people who do such things. Because many of these people had not met the girls or in some instances had not seen them for a long time, we wanted to include a recent photograph of each of them in their funeral cards. The film in their cameras had been developed and there was a delightful shot of Dani looking up at Roy as they rode a cable car up the ski slopes near Roy's sister's house. In the photo, Roy is looking directly into the camera and smiling his Norman Rockwell smile. Their expressions reveal their joy in each other and in life. There were several photos of Dawn that we could have used, but the best were taken with her nephew, and we didn't want his picture on a funeral card. We chose the one of her waiting to open her presents on her last Christmas morning. The ceramic Nativity scene made by her grandmother and given to her mother is visible behind her. She is smiling like every child smiles on Christmas morning. Even the funeral cards reminded me of birth announcements and baby pictures.

We came home from the mortuary to find that Mary Lou and Gordon were about to leave to drive to Los Angeles to pick up Pete's middle sister, Gina. She and her daughter and granddaughter had left home without enough money for the commuter hop from Los Angeles to Bakersfield and wanted someone to come get them. My in-laws had delegated Mary Lou and Gordon. I quietly informed them that they were not going. I needed them here, and that road was dangerous, and

I could not bear for anyone to leave here to drive on it for four hours. There was a bus that could pick Gina and her daughter and granddaughter up at the airport and deliver them to downtown Bakersfield. They could ride that. With that bloody navy blue purse beside me, I began to try to page Gina in the LA airport. I never did get her; she finally called back to see what was happening and was instructed to catch that bus and get here on her own. Never burden or inconvenience the people walking in the shadows. Your duty is to take whatever share of the burden you can carry; your duty is to avoid drawing attention to yourself for anything but comfort. Comforting they can do; they know about needing to be comforted. But they can't do you favors and clean up after you and be responsible for you. Don't ask them to.

At dusk Pete and I went out to the mortuary to check the viewing room and to visit our daughters' bodies. I had a very clear impression as I walked down the hall to that room. I was aware that those two girls were in there, laughing, giggling, criticizing, critiquing. I knew that when they heard our footsteps, they had, with dancing eyes, cried, "Quick, into the boxes. Lie still. Play dead." I could still hear the echoes of their giggles as I entered the room. I was certain they had just stopped moving, just as they so often did, years before, when I caught them playing in their room when they were supposed to be napping.

Pete walked slowly toward the two caskets. They were arranged so that the girls' feet were toward each other. We had ordered giant bridal bouquets for them. Dani's was white and loaded with dogwood. Dawn's was rose, her favorite color, and had dogwood and roses. They were graceful and beautiful and bridal. I watched Pete stop and stand with the palm of each hand touching a casket. His chin was tilted up; his eyes were closed. I think he was praying and I know he was suffering.

36

There weren't very many flowers. I began to fuss and asked Jim if I should order some to make the room look better. He smiled his funeral director smile and assured me that the flowers would be coming. "But we suggested donations in lieu of flowers!"

"That makes absolutely no difference. I don't care how loudly you say no flowers; people will send flowers."

He hadn't closed his mouth when there was a knock on the door and the florist began to carry in arrangements. We were relieved and gratified. We checked the cards and felt a special love for each person who sent those flowers. We carefully placed each bouquet around the room. As we worked, the door opened. Becky and Ken, Pete's little sister and her husband, had arrived. They studied us; they hugged; they were reassured. They walked tentatively toward those glowing wooden boxes. They stood with one hand on each casket and sobbed. Everyone did that; everyone placed their open palms on those boxes. People patted the boxes. There seemed to be a kind of comfort being exchanged as they caressed those oak and cherry containers of the corpses of those loving, laughing sprites.

Dottie called as soon as we were back home. Dottie and her husband, Fax, and Pete and Debbie were people I had met through work in the Tri-Cities. They were special friends, people of talent and intelligence, whom I enjoyed and admired greatly. "Bev, are you all right?" I assured Dottie that I was okay. She said, "Pete and Debbie will call you later. We are going over there in a little while. Rich Emery called us and told us. We are so sorry."

Pete and Debbie did call. They wanted to hear the whole story. They were positive, friendly, interested, and sympathetic, but not sad. They said, "We are fixing you a special package. It is an upbeat condolence gift. You will love it." I thanked them for an upbeat condolence call. When the box arrived, we were amazed at their whimsy and sensitivity. It was full of individually wrapped fruits, each one with a sticker or a happy face or a crinkly ribbon adorning it. There were walnuts, a coconut, oranges, bananas, and apples—each wearing a smiling face or a bright bow. We giggled and congratulated ourselves on having friends who could sympathize and smile. They were like a flotation collar thrown to a drowning person; with friends like these, we knew we could make it.

The house began to fill up. Meals appeared and disappeared. We did not eat. People made trips to delicatessens. Other people made lists of those who brought food and in what dishes. Thoughtful people labeled their containers; the most thoughtful people used disposable trays and plates. The most welcome foods were those that could be eaten with fingers. People did not seem to want to sit down to a dinner; they wanted to snack. The relish trays and cold-cut trays and breakfast rolls were especially popular. The day of the funeral, the ham and the salads made a lovely buffet, with Dani's egg salad and tuna salad garnishing the table. My brother arrived; my Aunt Lois arrived; Dawn's friends hugged and talked and made themselves at home. Each promised to tell his or her story the next day. We arranged for everyone to have juice and fruit and rolls at the house and then ride together in the limousines and our two Lincolns to the funeral. We would leave at 10 o'clock. Every one was relayed to the motel. Gordon had taken charge of transportation, and we were subliminally aware that people's needs were being met in his quiet and thorough way. Becky and Ken were here now, and that meant that sixteen-year-old Darcy had her eighteen- and fifteen-year-old cousins to share her bed on this night. They moved in all their luggage and hair dryers and sleeping bags and, by their presence and with their clutter, comforted Darcy.

Dawn's friends were going to sleep in her apartment. Her roommate still lived there and would act as host. They told me later that they spent almost the entire night going through Dawn's scrapbooks and diaries and photo albums. I was to discover that Dawn and Dani had chronicled their lives. They had every scrap of paper, every birthday card, every note, every calendar; it was all there. Their friends were flattered to find how they were valued and preserved in these books. I thanked God for this posthumous gift of the girls' treasures all preserved and catalogued, even down to descriptions of the weather, the music on the radio, their loves, their duties, and their dreams at specific moments in their history.

Roy's mother called several times during the weekend. She wanted Roy's dress blues buried with Dani. She had contacted San Diego, and they were finding his other pair and would send them Federal Express to the funeral home. She said they were married now; they were together forever. The navy would be flying Roy's ashes home in a special flight, which they were calling a training flight. His best friend, who had joined the service with him, would be sent as escort. The local paper would cover the arrival of the plane. People from their small town in Michigan were flooding them with food and flowers and visits. She said she was glad it was below freezing there, because she could use the back porch as a refrigerator for all that food. Over the phone, two women who had never met loved each other and worked together to bury their children.

CHAPTER THREE

The morning of the celebration. We woke; we wept; we dressed. I wore my diamond earrings and the outfit that Dani and I bought for me to wear at the rehearsal dinner when I first dined with her new in-laws. I was the mother of the bride; I was making a celebration and ceremony for my daughters. Everyone was dressing, the atmosphere only a little less festive than it had been when we dressed for Debra's wedding. Hair dryers growling, bathroom doors opening and closing, steam escaping. "How do I look?" "Is this all right to wear?" Front door open to the warm sun and soft, clean breeze. People drifting out to the patio. Dani and I had stained that redwood furniture early in February. We had dug up all the flower beds and put in bedding plants. We had thought we were doing it for the wedding and planned and dreamed and schemed as we worked. Now the patio and entry walkway were fresh and pretty; we had simply misunderstood the occasion for which we prepared them.

The limousines arrived. Someone had washed our cars and they were in line. The pastor had not yet arrived. We all drifted out and began to assign people to cars. It was amazing how many people needed to be close to us. We were somehow generating confidence. We were smiling. We were relaxed. People needed that touchstone. We decided to leave without the pastor. The four cars pulled away from the curb and moved slowly to the corner. The pastor was just approaching as we pulling into the main street. He circled and fell in behind our procession. We drove in the sunshine through town and along freeways and into the country. The cemetery and mortuary were at the very edge of town, only empty fields and foothills beyond.

Bird song and sunshine and soft, friendly winter breezes welcomed us as we stepped from the cars. Guests were standing across a driveway from us. No one started forward; they seemed frightened of us. I instructed our group to go greet them. We began to mingle. We laughed about my diamond earrings. I told the woman who worked in Dawn's office and who had shared in the Christmas fun when I got my ears pierced and then informed Pete that I was very poor at fractions and would have to have full carats to fill these newly acquired holes in my head that if you couldn't wear your new diamond earrings to your own daughters' funeral, where could you wear them? We thanked some of the people for coming, especially those strangers who had taken the time to go to the viewing room and sign that guest book. We searched out and hugged those who needed it; we also searched out and got hugged by those who we needed. We were standing between the rose garden and the mortuary; the open graves were beyond the rose garden. We had specified that there would be no awning over them. The sun shone on them, purifying that newly exposed soil. The hills beyond them were framed in crystal blue winter skies. There was bird song.

The doors to the mortuary were closed. We began to edge toward them. People followed us. At the door, I told them that it was a very large room and we were a small group, so please all stay together and sit at the front of the room. Then we opened the doors and heard the beautiful, almost celestial music that had been Dawn's favorite, saw Jim and an assistant standing just inside the door holding the funeral

41

cards, noticed flowers on stands in the back and front of the room, and were drawn to the glowing wooden boxes under the bridal bouquets at the front of the hall. Pete, Darcy, and I and Debra and her boyfriend Dennis sat in the front row. Dawn's good friend, Mike, and Darcy rolled the piano into position while Rich, who had been standing at the podium, returned to his seat. There followed a quiet period while people became accustomed to being there with those boxes and while some people meditated.

Then I signaled Rich and he introduced himself and explained the format of the service, inviting any and all to talk, explaining that we would be grateful for attempts, even if tears interrupted. He walked to his seat; almost without pause, I stood and walked a few steps to Dani's casket. Touching it, caressing it, I said, "I want to explain to you what you are looking at here. Dani is in this box. It is cherry because she loved antiques and had a cherry desk. Dawn is in this one. It is oak because she had an oak drafting table and because she was so involved with the oak trim at the racquet club. The flowers are supposed to be bridal bouquets because we thought this was as close as they would ever come to having bridal bouquets. Dani is dressed in her wedding dress. Because her head was not any longer the shape of a human head, we placed her tiara in her left hand. Roy's dress blues are tucked in beside her at the request of his mother. Dawn [and I stepped around a bouquet of white, long-stemmed roses and patted Dawn's casket, letting the energy flow from it into my hand] is wearing the new Liz Claiborne outfit she wore to San Francisco last weekend when she went to see the Vatican Exhibit. We hope she had a wonderful time in it and that she thought she was beautiful in it.

"I am going to tell you about Dani because Dawn has many friends here today who will talk about her and about her life. Dani's friends are in the navy, stationed in Florida, and unable to come here for this ceremony. They will hold a memorial service tomorrow at the base chapel. The orders of the day today more than suggest that contributions be made in Roy's and Dani's names to the Special Olympics because both of them worked hard for that charity, even planning and implementing a Special Olympics event on the base at Pensacola. I want to tell you how Dani came to be here today. She was discharged from the navy on December 24, 1983. She could have come home for Christmas but opted to stay and have Christmas in her home there. She called me and asked if I would like to drive across the States with her when she moved home; I was delighted. She sold her Toyota Celica, paid off her bills, and put $2,700 into the navy education fund to pay for her own college education. This act of independence was Roy's idea; he didn't want his new in-laws paying for his wife's education. I arrived January 13, 1984. The movers had been there that day and the apartment was empty and clean. The little red Volkswagen she had purchased for $500 was waiting at the motel they had rented for us. The back seat had been removed and a piece of plywood cut to fit in order to bring all of her houseplants with us to California. We left the next day, headed north through Georgia by the back roads and then to North Carolina to visit relatives and look for a piece of property to buy. Just before we arrived in North Carolina, we were struck by the thought that neither California nor Arizona would allow us to bring all those house plants into their states. We made a gift of them to our cousin and were able to spread our luggage a little thinner on the back seat platform area. We visited a few days, purchased the sixty-acre piece of Smoky Mountains that my grandfather had once owned and then drove west. At Oklahoma City, we hit below zero weather with ice and snow. The little Volkswagen had a heater that only worked on one side of the car, my side, and then only when the handle was held up. We froze! Pow-

43

dered snow blew in the defroster vent; icy air came in the hole in the door where a speaker was supposed to be. We wore almost everything we owned in an attempt to keep warm and then covered ourselves with a blanket. Dani's feet were freezing so she removed one boot at a time and I held it over the one heater vent to warm it and then traded her for the cold one. Ice formed on the inside of the windows; we often had to stop and spray deicer inside, wait for the air to clear, and then drive on. At Albuquerque, we quit; we could travel no farther with our coats buttoned over our heads and our breath freezing on the windshield. After a couple of failed attempts, we finally found a dealer who could wire the heater open. We drove out of town with the windows open, heat blasting from every orifice in that car.

"Dani and I toured the lower United States: Tennessee, Arkansas, Oklahoma, Texas, New Mexico, Arizona, and then home to California. We passed up the Grand Canyon because we were getting anxious to be home. When we arrived, Pete, Dawn, and her roommate were down at the boat for the weekend; they came home when we called them.

"We settled into a routine. It was such a delight to have Dani's company. We exercised, dieted, shopped; we went to Disneyland for a weekend with Dawn and Darcy. We worked in the yard and we pieced a beautiful Grandmother's Flower Garden quilt. Then Roy called. Would Dani come back and drive across with him? Dani asked her father's permission, because he had pronounced as edict that any daughter living with her lover before marriage would pay for her own wedding. Dani did not want to pay for her own wedding. Would Dad make a little exception for traveling together for one week? With averted eyes and a slight smile, he allowed as how he would.

"With a new dress and shoes and bag—not her usual little white one—a new haircut and manicured nails, Dani left

44

to meet Roy and surprise him a day early by attending his graduation from his special school. She arrived just at the end of the ceremony; photographs indicate his ordeal in maintaining his position on the field until he could get to her. That film was still in their cameras when they died. They drove to Colorado and visited Roy's sister and then drove home. Roy spent the weekend with us and then went to his new station in San Diego. We spent part of that weekend planning a wedding at the kitchen table. Pete and Roy decided that they would wear blue jeans and ruffled shirts, after they read *Miss Manner's Guide to Excruciatingly Correct Behavior* and discovered that that was the uniform for the boy you don't want your daughter to marry. We ignored them. Dani began tearing pages out of bride magazines and making lists. Roy left and Dani and I returned to our roadwork. I would ride along beside her, yelling encouragement such as, "Your cellulite is jiggling" while she pounded down the pavement. She met with the priest and reserved our twenty-eighth wedding anniversary as their wedding day. She and Roy had long discussions over the phone about this priest and his requirements that they attend a retreat for engaged couples. Roy was sure he didn't want to go there if they were going to talk about sex. It was just none of their business. Then it was Friday and Roy was here and they were together. They picked up Dawn, drove to meet the man who was so drunk that he crossed the center line and killed them.

"There is one more thing I want to say. Many of you have made the comment that you either don't believe there is a God because he wouldn't have done such a thing or have wondered at his cruelty. Please don't. There is a God. He is all there is. He created this universe and it is a lawful universe. That lawfulness produces a rhythm. These girls were in touch with that rhythm and they left when they were supposed to leave. Dani was first and that is how it should be. Dawn was

45

always a timid little girl, afraid of her own shadow. Dani was a brave little thing and helped her little sister through the rough spots. Dawn always said that she was never afraid to go to school, because Dani was there showing her the room and telling her all about the teacher and the subject matter. And that is how it is now. Dani was there saying, "Right over this way, Dawn. Right over here." And so, please, don't leave here shaking your fist in God's face. God didn't do this to us. Somehow, we do these things to ourselves. It is exactly as it should be; it is okay. And, now, please continue the conversations we have had in our kitchen the last few days. Please share with us the stories about these girls. Don't worry that you can't finish. Just start."

And they did. Dawn's high school friend and college roommate for two years, Terry, described the trip home for Christmas in her car with the broken door tied shut with a rope. The driver's door was frozen shut, so the only way in and out of that car was through the window on the driver's side. As they pulled into a service station for gas, Dawn said, "Terry, look at that gas pump. It is weird." It was beginning to swell and dance and then exploded just as they parked by it. Terry was laughing so hard that she was immobilized. Dawn couldn't get out her door because it was tied shut, so she snaked her five-foot–eleven-inch frame over Terry's contorted body and out through the window and captured the writhing gas hose, filled the tank, writhed back through the window, and they drove away.

Terry's husband, Robert, told of his amazement at Dawn's way of traveling. They live in San Francisco; Dawn visited them several times, including the last weekend she spent on earth. She would call them to say that she was in town and would be arriving at their house soon. He would ask if he should come down to the freeway and meet her. She always refused, but it would be hours before she would arrive. The

46

reason? She would not use the map and was determined to find the entrance to the tunnel that led to their neighborhood on her own. She just drove around until she happened on it. He turned to her roommate and asked, "Did she own a map?" The answer was, "I bought her many; she wouldn't use them." Robert said that Dawn would leave their apartment in the morning and walk all day in the city. At night, he would ask her to show him where she had been. Then he would tremble as he realized that she had walked alone through parts of the city where he would not go with an armed escort and a police dog. She had sensed no danger and, for her, there had been none.

Liz, darling little Liz, Dawn's good friend of five years, stood by the shining casket, rubbed and patted it, and talked about finals, and dinner parties, and diets, and trips, and her love for her friend. She seemed to be looking through the wood at her friend as she said good-bye and teased Dawn once more about her expensive teeth. Dawn had flown over the handlebars of the bicycle she got for her seventh birthday and knocked out her permanent front tooth. It had been re-implanted but fell out again on the day of her first prom. A flipper was hastily devised by a kindly dentist who would work on Saturday rather than let her miss her first formal dance. Then there had been braces with a false tooth fastened in the front and finally caps for the front teeth. Outgrown flippers could be found in little boxes in her apartment; she never parted with a thing, especially not her expensive teeth.

Dawn's sometime lover and all-time friend, Craig, wore Topsiders and a casual shirt to the funeral. Pete had commented on how these young kids dress for a funeral. Craig rose to explain that this shirt and these shoes had been Dawn's Christmas present to him and he had worn them to honor her on this day. He reminded us of the time they made a taxi sign for our Ford Escort, which Dawn had borrowed, and drove around campus picking up students in their pseudotaxi. He leaned toward us conspiratorially and said, "I think you ought to know how Dawn spent your money while in college. She gave dinner parties." He said that the check would arrive and she would have everyone over for a gourmet feast. Then it was back to beans and rice for three weeks.

Dawn's roommate described that last trip to San Francisco the weekend before in the little red Volkswagen. Since it was Dani's car, Dawn felt responsible and wouldn't allow anyone else to drive it. She did not bother to explain or to take into consideration the fact that she really couldn't drive a car with a standard transmission. As they began their assault on the hills of the city, he pleaded to be allowed to drive. "No, this is Dani's car and I am not letting anyone else drive it." He finally got down on the floor and worked the pedals with his hands in order to assure their safe progress through the city. He said that they had been congenial roommates: "She did the laundry and I cooked." As he went on to say that they had never fought, I heard Dawn confiding to me, as she had many times, "He is being a butt today." He was lying, but he probably needed to remember it that way.

Then Aunt Becky walked to the front and stood between the two boxes and sobbed, "I am their Aunt Becky. I am the emotional one." While people chuckled sympathetically, she regained her composure and talked about the girls, visits to her house, sleeping on the floor in sleeping bags, the Thanksgivings together, and practical jokes played on Uncle Ken and on Dawn's college friends, brought along on trips to Portland to bunk on her floor. Aunt Becky talked of her love for them and for us, their parents, and of her respect for the parenting we had done with those girls. She said she had always used us as an example of how to be good parents. Those words were very welcome at a time when one cannot help wondering if one made their lives all they could have been. Then Aunt

Becky's daughter Tina introduced herself and remembered summer visits and swimming in the pool and giggling all night. Tami, Tina's sister, the other cousin, stood, looking so vulnerable, and described the joy of having Dawn and Dani as cousins, the fun they had together on holidays and summer vacations. Their grandmother stood up and expressed her pride in her family.

Then the girls' father walked to the front. I was startled. Pete was going to talk at his daughters' funeral, Pete the strong, silent type, Pete who could not cry in public and rarely cried in private, Pete who loved without words, but with deeds. He told of his joy in his adult daughters and of a visit Dani made to a job site in Oklahoma that provided them the opportunity to spend a weekend alone together. They had talked and talked, sharing dreams and plans and memories. And he spoke of his pride in Dawn's work for him and for others as an architect and of their closeness as they learned from each other and shared the pleasure of creating a good building as inexpensively as possible. He described the trip he and Dawn made from Washington State to Bakersfield in a heat wave with no air-conditioning. And then he explained that he and our entire family felt that the girls' deaths were as it should be, that it was all right.

Then the girls' little sister, Darcy, spoke of her love for her sisters. She turned to Debra and said, "I am so glad you didn't go with them on Friday. I couldn't have stood losing you, too." Debra sobbed aloud.

Now new friends and acquaintances began to talk. Mark, the boy who sat on the bed and taped the music for the funeral, told of taking Dawn to a company picnic at which her antics and intolerance of pomposity made the company president smile for the first time in living memory. Gene, a business associate of Pete's, talked about watching the family together and going to dinner with all of us. Paula, who worked at the

49

next desk from Dawn, talked about the tape. Every time that Dawn tore the tape off of a drawing, she would wad it up and throw it at Paula. Paula had tried not to react, but her annoyance had been revealed by a twitching muscle in her jaw, which Dawn spotted and used as a scorecard. Paula saved all the tape. At Christmas, she bought a little brass bowl with a lid, placed the ball of tape pieces in that bowl, and wrapped it. Dawn, who collected brass, was delighted with the gift. As she oohed and aahed, Paula said, "No, Dawn, open it!" Dawn did. Then Paula inclined her body toward me and asked, "Shall I say it?"

"Go ahead," I said.

She said, "Dawn yelled, 'You turd!' and threw it at me." (I later found that ball of tape in Dawn's box of Christmas decorations, carefully preserved with the obvious intention of giving it back to Paula next Christmas. I took it to the office and tossed it to Paula. She kept it.)

Don, Dawn Marie's boss, talked about her professional attire and behavior, about her skill and discipline, and about their names. When she first went to work for him, the similar names caused confusion. Dawn rather timidly suggested that her family called her Dawnzie. Don was charmed by that confession; her name at work became Dawnzie, except to clients. Then she was Dawn Marie. He said her desk would be filled, her chair would have another occupant, but no one would ever take Dawn Marie's place in their office or in their hearts.

Now Mike rose. He and Dawn had been such dear friends, and he allowed us to watch that friendship develop as he described early classes, climbing Mount Rainier, swimming in Lake Tonasket, and hosting our table at the Symphony Ball when we left to be with Deb when she was in labor with our first grandchild. He mentioned the last November weekend visit to Aunt Becky's and his and Dawn's sleeping

50

on the living room floor and driving to the Oregon coast. He said, "I didn't know Dani very well, but we spent that Saturday night making radish rosettes for Nana and Baba's golden wedding anniversary celebration and I enjoyed talking with her." Then he walked to the piano.

Darcy was waiting for him there. She said, "This is the song Dani wanted me to sing at the wedding reception. We hadn't yet chosen the music for the ceremony. For some reason, I knew that I needed to get this song learned. Now I understand; I will sing it for her now." She stood by that piano and sang like a trouper, like a professional, her voice never breaking. Mike accompanied her and then sang the last chorus with her. She sat down beside him on the piano bench.

Mike turned toward the audience and said, "When Bev called me and told me that Dani and Dawn were dead, my parents and I were preparing a dinner party for friends. After dinner, I sang a few songs for our guests. I told them of Dawn's death and said that I would sing this song for her: 'The Shadow of Your Smile.'" The words were perfect and his love for her was evident as he sang. Mike and Darcy rose and walked to Pete and me and both children embraced us.

The Reverend Gordon went to the podium; he spoke of his joy in this celebration, of having learned to know the girls as we talked today. He read Scriptures and poetry that he had chosen, each choice perfect and exactly what we would have chosen. He prayed and then reminded everyone that we would walk to the grave site and that the caskets would be lowered while we watched. As he left the podium, I offered those who wanted them the white long-stemmed roses that stood in a vase between the two caskets. Several people came and got a rose to throw into the graves.

Mike and Craig and Dawn's roommate and her Uncle Ken and her boss, Don, and her friend from work, Paul, went about the business of carrying out one casket and then returning for the other. We all watched, much as one watches a recessional at a wedding. People were busy getting flowers to take to the graves; they broke blossoms off funeral arrangements. We followed the last casket up the aisle and walked into the sunlight. My brother offered me his arm; my aunt walked beside me. Pete brought up the rear. We strolled along the rose garden, down a lane through the graves, up a road, and then across the grass and up a hill to those graves. As we walked, we watched the cars being filled with flowers and then moving across the top of the hill to the graves. The men once again carried those heavy boxes and balanced them on the ropes stretched across the grave openings.

There were chairs there, but no one sat in them. We were busy. We were burying our dead. The Reverend Gordon read the traditional Scripture and then was handed a poem which Megan, another of Dawn's co-workers, had given to me as we neared the graves. It was one that had comforted her when her grandfather died and was intended as a love-note to Dawn Marie and as a comfort to those who mourned her. It began "When I die . . ." and ended "at least let me live in your eyes/And not on your mind." She had signed it and added "I love you, Dawn Marie." He read the poem; the service ended.

It was after noon and the sun was high in the sky. Two men dressed in wash pants and ill-fitting sport coats began to ready the machinery for lowering the caskets. They were self-conscious; I wished I had thought to tell Jim that they did not need to be dressed in anything but their usual work clothes. They sweated. We crowded forward; we were in their way. We wanted to be near them and watch that it was done as it should be. Just as Dani's casket was settled on the bottom, a plane passed overhead. Mary Lou, who is a pilot and sensitive to planes passing overhead, looked up and said,

"Bev, that is a helicopter. That is for Dani." Then Dawn's casket was lowered. There was no further ceremony. We crowded close and looked down into the graves. Mike threw in a letter that had been delivered to Dawn's house the day after she died, one he had written and waited to send until he could also return a book he had found among his things that belonged to her. He sent it with her now. Flowers were thrown in. Darcy kneeled and dropped those giant bridal bouquets, first into Dani's grave—her bouquet landed squarely at the head of the casket—and then into Dawn's—once again a perfect landing at the head of the box. Then Darcy dragged an asymmetrical flower arrangement over to Dawn's side. I commented that that was appropriate because Dawn had an asymmetrical haircut. We just stood in the sun, aware of the soft little clouds floating near the mountains, of the breeze, of the bird song, and of the warmth of the sun. We talked quietly. We didn't want to leave. Then someone's stomach growled. I said, "Come on, everyone, let's go eat." All together we walked down the hill to the waiting cars and piled in. We left without looking back. We had said good-bye. I felt like a tired mother-of-the-bride after a wedding that had gone off without a hitch. I had made a good ceremony for my daughters and I was proud and satisfied.

As we drove, we visited. The little red Volkswagen had definitely been eulogized. I teased the roommate that it wasn't entirely true that he and Dawn had never fought; he informed me that one didn't admit those things at a funeral. We commented on who had been there. We were at peace. We were proud of ourselves. I said that I was so proud of Dawn's friends, who they were, and what they were, and that they had been able to make this ceremony what it had been. Jim told us that the dress blues arrived just ten seconds before we opened the doors to walk into the hall, that he had kicked the wrapper into a closet and had just closed the coffin lid when

53

we entered. Roy's mother would be so pleased that they were there. Dani was pleased, too. I knew that both girls were very proud of us and the funeral we had made for them.

At the house, people pitched in and food was soon displayed on the dining room table. People sat around the living room and on the patio. Debra had three boyfriends there; they were rather evenly spaced around the available territory, but she sat with Dennis. Pete sent some of the boys after our grandson, who was at a day care center. We needed his innocence and beauty.

He was not innocent, however. He brought me a book to read. As I explained that the monkey was very sad because of some event in the story, he raised his little face and, with a worried expression, studied the face of his grandfather. He knew we were sad. He knew why. Debra had heard him, in his crib that morning, have a long conversation with his aunt Dani and his aunt Dawn. Babies are quite familiar with the place and can move freely between here and there.

After several hours, people began to leave. Dawn's friends went over to Debbie's apartment to sit in the hot tub and empty the liquor cabinet, with my blessing. My brother and aunt stayed with us, as did Becky and Ken and Pete's other sister, Gina, and her daughter and granddaughter. It was night. Someone started to rummage in the refrigerator to find food for the group. I said, "Let's return to normal. Come on, let's go out to dinner." We divided up and got into cars and went to a local restaurant. I was very tired; the strength that had sustained me for the last three days was not available to me now because there was nothing that I had to do. The video screen was filled with a raunchy rock group; the conversation drifted to pornography. I related the one experience Pete and I had had in a porno shop and our disappointment with the movie we had purchased guiltily and smuggled home. Pete began to fidget; I was out of line. One doesn't talk about pornography hours after burying one's daughters. We finished eating and left the restaurant, changing the subject without any obvious damage to anyone's dignity. But another lesson was about to be learned.

As you begin to walk in that place, people who are good and sensitive and who respond to their very best instincts reach out to help you. During the time between the deaths and the funeral, one comes to rely on that goodness, but, like Christmas, it doesn't last. The funeral was over; the hiatus was also over. Now it was okay to be jealous and to be snide and to frolic among the wounded. We are strong people who are normally well defended from pettiness and jealousy. Our defenses were down and those who are not strong, would not normally storm our battleworks, came out to poke and prod and wound, like hyenas after the kill. A niece raced home to tell her grandparents about the nasty story I had told about a porno movie. She informed them that it was so bad that she had had to leave, which was a lie. Pete's father, who is very skilled at making "you and him fight," began to work his craft. He was sleeping at Debra's, but he stayed at my house during much of the day. He carried tales of actions and conversations between the two houses. We were not ourselves; we did not evaluate what he was saying. We did not question him or stop him because we felt that surely no one would willingly add more pain at this time in our lives. Debra became more and more withdrawn; she did not look healthy. Finally, she began to see a mental health professional. Her mourning was not progressing normally. We did not even suspect the cause of her trauma. We had not yet learned that mourning is not a safe thing to do; we didn't yet know about the hyenas.

CHAPTER FOUR

People left to catch planes and to begin long drives back to their homes or to vacation spots in Southern California. The florists kept coming; more and more plants and arrangements were placed on the patio. The weather was mild; the plants liked the environment out there. The mailman began leaving twenty or thirty cards and letters each day. I cried as I read, but I was sustained and supported by the contact with friends and acquaintances and the honor given to our daughters. I turned the dining room table into a writing desk, the same table where Dani and I sat just a week before and tucked the ends of yarn and crocheted and visited while we finished that afghan. I began to write thank-you notes for each letter and for each flower arrangement and for each kindly gesture. The first day after the funeral, with all the leave-takings and busyness, was tolerable. I wrote letters; I talked to Gloria on the phone about the funeral arrangements for Roy. They had a photo of Dani and Roy enlarged and placed on the altar. We sent flowers with dogwood in the arrangement, which was also placed on the altar. Because they were having Catholic services, there would be only the photo, the flowers, and a dedication of the mass; there would also be a short eulogy by a priest for whom Roy had served as altar boy.

There was a call from Theresa in Florida, telling us about the memorial service on the base. They had taped it; the tape arrived along with the funeral card for that service.

Whiting Field Chapel
Naval Air Station Whiting Field
1500
01 March 1984

The order of the service was delineated. On the opposite page, someone had written the details of their lives as garnered from their military files. The accompanying letter from their commanding officer mentioned their work with the Special Olympics and some other activities, like the semiannual rubber chicken contest that Dani had invented and which was now a base tradition. He didn't mention her activities as a narc. Dani hated narcotics and didn't want to fly with those people she knew were using them. She fed information to the commanding officer to make the urine checks more reliable by telling him when to take them. Several fellows are no longer in the navy because Dani played narc. I could hear Theresa's baby crying on the tape of the service.

A call came from the campus in Washington. Dawn's friends had held a memorial service for her and had written down what each person said, bound the pages like a book, and sent it to us. Michelle said, "But the most vivid reruns these past few days have been of when we would go to Alex's and discuss our mothers, and men, and our goals in life. A short note on these subjects: it is difficult now for us not to feel a frustrating helplessness when we think of Bev and Pete, Dawn Marie's mother and father. One of Dawn Marie's best friends, Michael Stanley, has told me that he will play the piano and sing this morning for them. Our support, even though we cannot be right with Dawn Marie's family, is the most valuable gift of life we can give." The Commanding Officer also sent along a typed copy of his eulogy for Dani. We were not surprised that a naval officer knew how

57

to deal with the bereaved parents, but how did these young people learn such wisdom and graciousness?

Two days after the funeral, Debbie called from the office. She said, "Dad, I am making decisions that I am not qualified to make. You are going to have to come back to work." She sounded shattered, drained, and very, very tired. Pete went back to work.

The numbness was wearing off. The pain was excruciating. I screamed to God in that voice that is not audible here but is heard very clearly there. I demanded that He help us. Pete and I have a guru; I hate to mention that word because it reeks of beads and the sixties and strange behavior on California beaches, but we do have a guru. I prayed to him, much as a Catholic prays to saints. I reminded him of his suffering when his mother died and when his own guru died; I told him that he had promised to care for and to guard us. I demanded protection and comfort. I stood in my living room, surrounded by familiar furniture and passing people, and internally screamed for help. It came. As I stood by the dining room table, looking at the stacks of flower cards, the thank-you cards, the pen, and the address books, arms reached around me from behind. I was lowered gently into my chair. I was permeated with love. The room filled with love. It was like a clear gelatin; it was palpable. It was warm; there was light. I was held, snuggled into the lap of God. Somehow I knew that Dani was involved. She too hugged and held and helped me sit and snuggle into protection and shelter and comfort and sustenance. My eyes filled with tears; I talked quietly to my loving Father-God. I thanked Him for strength and love. I walked peacefully in a house filled with the tangible presence of God's love.

I don't know when the vision came. It could have been the same day that God held me or it could have been the day after. It doesn't matter. I was suddenly aware that I was look-

58

ing at my guru standing with his arms around my two daughters and Roy. The space around them was royal blue; there was a golden ring around that space. I really didn't believe my eyes. I checked their relative heights. Yes, Dawn was taller than any of them; Roy and the Master were about the same height, and Dani was just a little shorter. She stood in front. They were all smiling at me, a gentle smile. Wordlessly, the kids were telling me not to make a scene, that they had it all in control, that the Master was tending to them. Somehow, they all looked more mature and wiser than I. I don't know how long I looked at them and they looked at me, but it was ended as suddenly as it began. I went on about my business. I commented to no one. These things happen in that other place and have nothing to do with this one.

Pete and I were both fussing about the need to talk to someone whose ideas were similar to ours. We called the main office of the group with which we worship. Yes, someone would see us. Who did we want that someone to be? We asked that we be allowed to visit with Anandamoy, a yogi and monk who is pastor of the Pasadena Church of Self-Realization Fellowship. He agreed to leave the afternoon open; we could meet with him whenever we arrived in Los Angeles. We already had an appointment at 1:00 with an attorney to make certain that we were free to dispose of our daughters' estates, that there would be no probate or some other such foolishness. Ruie and Mil, my in-laws, wanted to ride along with us to Los Angeles. We met the attorney, picked Ruie and Mil up, and drove directly to the Mother Center, as we call the national headquarters of Self-Realization Fellowship. A friend was walking up the driveway as we drove in. We stopped; she reached through the car window and hugged us. We were led to sofas in the main room. Another friend ran in to give us hugs. Anandamoy came as she was leaving to go outside and visit with Ruie and Mil while we talked with the yogi.

59

He wasn't sure what we wanted from him; neither were we. We told him a little about the accident. He said his brother was killed in a motorcycle accident and he knew how devastating the deaths of loved ones could be. I didn't relate to that because we did not feel devastated. He asked if we thought God had done this to us. I explained that God was not that kind of a God, that somehow we do these things to ourselves, that we have free will, that choices and actions have consequences, that . . . I looked up at him. He was smiling gently. He said, "Go on. You're doing fine." Yoga has existed for centuries, thousands of years. The Masters have found a way to walk with one foot here and the other in that other place. We asked how the Masters describe the place in which our girls now live. Anandamoy said that it is thought forms and light and color, that Dawn would love it there. I said that she was probably busy learning the names of all those colors now and redesigning heaven. He reminded me that she would only have to think it different and it would be. Then he gave the piece of advice for which we had come. He said, "You are still in shock. You are all right now but when this wears off, when all the tasks are done, you could begin to turn this energy inward, and that would be destructive. That energy turned inward becomes hate and anger. Do not do that. Every time you think of them, smile and send love." Those two words rang in my ears. Yes, of course, send love. He said that their personalities were still intact, that they were aware of our pain and would be aware of our love. I don't remember anything he said after that. I had heard what I needed to hear. Send love. Smile and send love.

Our friend Donna was crouched beside the car, talking through the window to Ruie and Mil, when we came out with Anandamoy. He left us to open the gate for us. We invited Donna to join us for dinner. She recommended a Thai restaurant she had discovered recently; we went there. As we began to order, I noticed that Pete was reluctant to order anything. It had been one week since he had eaten the fish and chips we had brought back to the boat for him. I told him to eat; he replied, "I can't. I was eating when they were dying."

"You were also breathing and swallowing and digesting when they died. You can't stop doing what you were doing then. They wouldn't want this of you. You eat."

He studied me for a minute and then ordered his meal. When the food came, we discovered that we had recovered our appetites. We were hungry!

We were surrounded by their possessions. Each shoe and each dress was precious because it served as a catalyst for remembering. One sunny day during our month together, a truck driver called the house and told Dani that he had made a mistake, had not read his bill of lading properly and had driven to Bakersfield instead of to Edwards Air Force Base with her household shipment. We met him at the storage warehouse and rescued Dani's clothes, the back seat of her car, and her yellow Schwinn bicycle from the things going into storage until her marriage in July. The bike was rusted from the humid sea air of Florida. We reminisced about that bicycle as we took it to the shop to be completely repaired and repainted. She reminded me that it had never been unscratched in all the time she had owned it. I had talked her into loaning it to a neighbor girl for a 100-mile bike trip the very first week she had owned it. Joyce had returned it to Dani scratched and never did make good on her promise to have it repainted. I marveled at what a mean mother I had been and told Dani, "You should have said no. You shouldn't have let me do that to you." And then I felt guilty. Grown up children have wicked memories.

I picked up the bike the week after Dani died. It looked pristine and new. We told the man who owned the shop that Dani would never get to see it. When we filled him in on some of the details, he said, "Oh, yes, I heard about that funeral. My brother-in-law went to it." He then took twenty-five dollars off the price of the repairs. We tried to stop him but he wanted to do something and that was something he could do.

Dani's shoes reminded me of the weekend we spent on the boat. Dani loved the boat and was excited about being aboard the *Beverly Ann* once again. The whales were migrating from Alaska to Mexico and people were calling each other on the marine radio to inquire for sightings of whale spumes. We cruised out of Ventura Harbor and headed for the islands, watching for whales every minute. Our little grandson was aboard, firmly tied into a life jacket and riding behind his grandfather in the captain's chair on the bridge. Dani and Darcy spotted something. "There's one! There's a whale!" I didn't think so. Whatever it was seemed to be floating on the surface and staying pretty much in one place.

"Dani, I don't think that is a whale," I told her.

She planted her size 7 tennis shoes firmly on the deck and said, "I'm here to tell you that that is a whale."

We headed for it. It was a long twig floating on the top of the water with a few sea gulls riding on it. "You're here to tell me that's a whale, huh?" For the rest of her life, we teased her about being here to tell us things.

Dani sorted her clothes. She was a keeper; some of these clothes were from the sixth grade. Some of the shoes should never have been purchased in the first place. Dani was never known for her taste. She was dainty and feminine, but would dress in clunky clodhoppers, blue jeans, and a T-shirt all the time if left to her own desires. We threw out some of those shoes. We gave the Salvation Army most of those sixth grade dresses. When she had all her clothes arranged in a metal closet in the garage, she counted twenty-two pairs of slacks. Some of them were as old as the hills, some were almost unworn because she had changed sizes soon after their purchase, but all were in very good condition. Dani took very good care of everything, even the dresses she purchased without a chaperone to guide her. She always bought dresses that made her look about forty-five and dowdy. When she came home for our last Thanksgiving together, she asked if she should buy the dress for her grandparents' fiftieth anniversary celebration before she came home. Every female member of the family chorused, "No!" Dani flew into Portland; we went directly to our favorite department store and outfitted Dani in a turquoise silk dress with hose and shoes to match. She looked twenty-five and elegant. She changed to a sweatsuit as soon as the festivities were over. She wasn't really comfortable looking twenty-five and elegant.

Dani's clothes were hanging in the closet. Her papers were neatly filed in the drawers. She had everything in order, as if she had been warned and had prepared herself and her effects for death. It was time for Ruie and Mil to go home. Since Dani and her grandmother were the same size, we went through the clothes. The shoes and slacks fit Ruie perfectly, and she took them. Some jackets and sweaters fit Darcy and me. We took them. Some things were so closely associated with Dani that we couldn't keep them. The Salvation Army stack grew higher and higher. Darcy took the underwear; Ruie took the bridal finery. We had had a lingerie shower for Dani's twenty-fifth birthday; she had preserved all that lace and satin for her marriage to Roy. Debbie reported that Ruie modeled it that night for Milford. We were at the beginning of a lengthy sorting process.

Both Dani and Dawn had their own completely furnished apartments. Dawn's roommate was still living in hers so it was too soon to begin the dividing and distributing there. Some things had already been given away. Dawn's friends had asked for something of hers and I had allowed them to choose from

63

among her box collection. Her roommate had even given away some of Dawn's clothes. Now Ruie wanted Dawn's old doll, Punkin. We went to her apartment to get it. Dawn's room was like a movie stuck in the projector, suspended in motion. The ironing board was still up. A letter was lying open on the dresser where she had tossed it when she came in from work on Friday night. The photos on the wall smiled at us. The knickknacks, each one with a known history, were grouped around the room. The book by the bed. Her reading glasses. We opened drawers and closets. Everything was in order, everything labeled and filed, just as if some doctor had said, "You have six months to live. Get your life in order." The girls' lives had been in order.

Ruie and Mil stopped by the house on their way out of town. As he walked to the kitchen table, Mil said, "Dawn knew that Debra was going to marry Dennis. She was going to stand up with her. They kept it a secret from you." Too late, defenses flew up. Too late. The hurt was done. Me, the eternal mother-of-the-bride, had a dead daughter who was not here to defend herself or to explain it away, who had planned to be her sister's bridesmaid and had not discussed it with me.

I did not change my facial expression. My father-in-law had hurt me, but he was not going to have the satisfaction of knowing it. I said something about the fact that Debra's plans for marriage changed every hour on the hour and that it was still not at all certain which of her three suitors would be her bridegroom and definitely not certain when she would be married. Ruie finished a project she had started earlier, and they left. As soon as they drove away. I began to cry—hard, loud crying. That hurt! And the pain taught one more lesson: don't ever tell the bereaved what the deceased said about them. They have no recourse. They can't check it out. You might have misunderstood. Just don't do it.

I cried simply because I needed to cry; there had always

64

been someone around and I had not had the opportunity to make noise and howl and keen. I cried noisily all day long. I waited for Deb to get home from work. We were going to talk about this. I needed to know why she would have told her grandparents that Dawn and she were keeping a wedding and all those wedding plans secret from me.

I called her. I confronted her. We yelled; we cried; we threatened to hang up; we talked; and, finally we understood. Oh, Lord, did we understand. It was so complicated. Debra was convinced that I had loved Dani and Dawn more than her and that I had loved Dani more than any of them. When she tried to criticize Dani soon after we returned from our journey, I stopped her. I told Debra that Dani was my only child with whom I never had to think about what I was going to say, the only one who was completely uncritical of me. Since Debra and Dawn were very busy at that time getting me raised to their high standards, that comment struck home. Now, she was trying to say that if Dani were mine, Dawn had been hers, that Dawn loved her best of all the sisters. And Milford had sensed this tangled web of emotions and pounced. Debra began to tell me the things he had said to her in her apartment at night after spending the day with me in my apartment. She told the tales he had carried from house to house.

As I responded, Pete came into the den. He had been listening. He was going to stop this conversation. We were not going to talk about his father this way. Then he began to weep. He knew it was true. All of his life he had witnessed his father doing that crafty stirring up of other people's emotions, that skillful let's-you-and-him-fight gamesmanship, that wily control of his family members by devious manipulation of their emotions. Pete had to accept the fact that his father had used this period of intense emotion to disrupt our family and to prevent Debra from availing herself of whatever comfort we could have offered her. Now we all wept quietly. We were still bruised, but we would heal. We had each other and we had love. And we would devise a strategy that would prevent Mil from having any further opportunity for his games. We would challenge his every statement with, "Did she tell you to tell me this? Then why are you telling it? What do you hope to gain?" We would turn every thrust into a counterthrust requiring either a quick exit or some self-examination for motives. I was sure we could count on the quick exit. We rested. We spoke quietly. We hung up.

I slept well that night. I got up, made the bed, fixed breakfast, took my shower, dressed, and started toward the typewriter in the den to continue writing the letters that needed to be written. As I entered the entry hall from the bedroom wing, I saw Dawn Marie come in the front door. She cocked her head and smiled at me as if to ask if it was all right that she was here. In that internally audible voice, I almost sang with joy as I said, "Oh, I am so glad to see you. Thank you for coming." I kept walking toward my typewriter, passing her. I could see her clearly but knew that she wasn't quite tangible: I could also see through her. I kept walking because I didn't really know the etiquette of this place. She followed me and then she reached out and *hugged* me. As I sat down at the typewriter, she joined me there and her body seemed to pass into mine. We were taking up the same space, and my body became very warm, as if the frequency at which the atoms of my body vibrated was accelerated and producing heat. And there was love. My child was hugging me, but we were operating at different vibration levels, hers much higher than mine. I thanked her for hugging me, for being there. And then we settled in. We were simply together. She was there all morning. I was not aware of her leave-taking; she was there and then she was not there. I understood that the confrontation with Debra had freed Dawn to come to me. Debra had needed her so much and had kept her, but now Dawn was free. Now she understood the dynamics of that last month of jostling for position as the three older sisters tried once again to find their places in the family, this time as independent adults who still needed to be loved the most. She understood. I understood. We could be together and then we could separate, now that we understood. I sat and thought about that sensation of heat. I felt it especially in the bend of my arms, along my chest and face. No, not on—in. My feet did not seem to be involved, but then who hugs feet? And so we finished our unfinished business in that place.

CHAPTER FIVE

Dani Lynn and Dawn Marie and Roy John died on Friday night, February 24, at 7:30 P.M. We did not know they were dead until Saturday morning. Tami and Tina arrived Monday to share Darcy's room. Sunday night Darcy was sleeping alone. In the middle of the night, she opened the door of our room and asked if she could sleep with us. She was sobbing. She crawled in on my side. I hugged and patted her.

"Oh, Mama," she cried, "they were there. I just wanted to know if they were still alive wherever they were. I asked them to come to me if they still existed. They came. Dani kneeled down on one side of the bed and held my hand and kissed it. Dawn stood on the other side and gently touched the back of my hand. They just looked at me and touched my hands."

"And you ran from them."

She sobbed in reply. Her father reached across my body and laid his arm on her and said, "You must not do that. You must not call them back. They must be free to go on and learn and grow and do the things they must do where they are."

I added, "They loved you so much that when you called them, they came back from where they are to comfort and reassure you. You ran from them. I hope they understand.

Darcy, do not call them back again. Do not make them worry about your problems. That is how one makes ghosts, by being so selfish that one does not let go." Her daddy began to talk about God and the astral plane on which we believe live those whose energy level is higher than ours. After a while, Darcy got sleepy and probably bored and went back to her own bed and to sleep.

This letting go became a topic of some discussion with several of Dawn's peers. Dani's friends were navy people who had been through several rigorous training camps and had looked at death from the seat of a training helicopter or from underwater or from inside a gas mask. They knew they were mortal and had come to terms with that fact. Dawn's friends had just graduated from college, were celebrating their first-quarter century, and still believed that dying was something only old people did and that somehow they had the secret that would keep them from ever getting old. When Dawn—lively, energetic, vivacious, bright, fun Dawn—could die, they were in jeopardy. The late night phone calls began soon after they returned home from the funeral. They said they wanted to talk about Dawn, that they were depressed and cried a lot, that people were expressing concern that they weren't getting over it rapidly. I was not sympathetic. I asked for whom they were really mourning, if it was not possible that they were staring at their own death. When they were ready to accept that, they didn't need to call anymore.

Terry called. Dawn had visited her on that last weekend in San Francisco. Dawn's roommate had been along. He was a fellow not much loved by his classmates. Dawn's friends had not been able to understand or forgive her for bringing him along to California with her. Terry had seen that look in Dawn's eyes that I had seen; she, too, had peered into the place, but she thought she was reading a look that said, "*If only he wasn't here, we could talk. I really need to talk to you*." Terry was playing If Only. I sternly reminded her that Dawn had always done exactly what she wanted to do. She needed that not–so–well–loved fellow to build a bridge between her college campus and her new life out in the real world, as she called it. Not every young man would be willing to tag along and play at being Dawn's bridge. And she must have wanted him along on that trip to San Francisco or he wouldn't have been there. No one made Dawn do anything she didn't want to do. And, if Dawn had wanted to talk, they would have talked. Terry had misinterpreted that look, and she was not to play If Only.

We live in a world of cause and effect. Every choice, every action, has a consequence. And the little consequences add up to big ones. I am not sure that there is anything governing our choices, except maybe our own earlier choices. There is such a strong sensation or intuition that Dani and Dawn came into this life together, knowing what it was they had to accomplish and then, having done so, left together. I do not mean they were fated to die at a certain time in a certain place, but that they were part of a lawful universe in which certain actions result in certain reactions, which led them to that spot in the road at exactly the same time as a poor man from Mexico who was out of work and had had too much to drink arrived at that spot in the road. If one looks backward from that bloody, noisy moment, one is dazzled, dazed, intoxicated by the millions and billions of tiny decisions that led those four young people to be exactly there exactly then. In the face of that myriad decision points, which one will you change? If only someone had run back up the stairs to get something. If only someone had had to go to the bathroom along the way. If only someone had decided to get a cup of coffee. No. The borders of that place extend way beyond that spot in the road or that moment in time. The voice in the corner in August had known and prepared our

70

family for their leave-taking. Dani's death was already happening when I dreamt of her in her wedding dress. Dani somehow knew she would never wear that diamond engagement ring; she mourned that fact as we drove home from the jewelry store. Dawn allowed me to look into eternity through the holes in her skull that had once been eyes. Dani kept fading in and out in my kitchen. At another level of our being, possibly a superconscious one, we know when we approach the boundaries. Once all the decisions have been made, once the chain of events has been set in motion, all the little If-Onlys cannot stop it. If someone had stopped for a cup of coffee, the man from Mexico would have stopped for another drink. Those four people were involved in an intricate dance, bobbing and weaving their way to that moment which existed inside and outside of time and space. It was an immutable event, selected from all possible events by millions of actions and reactions. If Only is a silly game that makes naive mourners suffer. One must not play it.

Ben called. Ben did not come to the funeral. He had attended too many funerals. His mother died last winter of cancer. His father died when Ben was younger. His niece was killed in a car wreck in January. Too many funerals. Ben didn't need to come to a mortuary in Bakersfield to begin his mourning; he was well practiced and could do it where he was. He sent a pencil drawing his mother had done of a broken swing on a grassy dune. She called it *Fond Memories*. I had it matted in soft grays and hung it near Dawn's graduation picture in the guest room. Ben is only twenty-five, but he is old. I remember the day that I got old. I was standing in the doorway of our house in suburbia, looking out at the cul-de-sac, watching the neighborhood children play. My three toddlers were behind me in the room. My twenty-fifth birthday was just days away. Suddenly it struck me that I could die—not that I would die, just that I could. And then I was mature.

71

Dawn gave those of her friends who were willing to accept it a gift. She gave them the gift of maturity. Ben didn't need it; he already had it.

The intense emotional experience, the openness and freedom of communication with others, the lack of defenses—one doesn't use them here because they haven't served as a real protection from anything and the energy needed to guard the fortress is better used in healing the tears in the fabric of one's reality—all cooperate to create a high that lasts for several weeks. One could become addicted to this high—it is a powerful psychedelic drug. And there are those who are addicted to it: letters come from strangers who have lost children. They give their phone numbers and ask you to call. I wonder that they don't pick up the phone and dial. They have left the mountaintop and envy you your position on it. They are attempting a vicarious reentry into that secret kingdom at the top of the hill. It won't work; they can't come back in, and you can't stay. One must begin a gradual descent without descending too far.

I understand the temptation, though. A month after the girls died, a little schoolmate of Darcy's was killed while riding on a motorcycle with her boyfriend. I rushed to their house with a disposable tray filled with vegetables and dip. I went to the funeral home to sign the book in the viewing room. I wanted to talk to them to give them all the wonderful benefit of my experience. Thank God, I missed them. I realized what I was doing before the funeral and did not attend. I sent a card, sharing the yogi's words. That was the only gift I could give. I needed to leave the valley of the shadows; the joy and the love and the intense emotion were no longer mine. I should be busy controlling the speed and distance of my descent. They would find their way. I would not become a funeral junkie. I would let go—of my daughters, of the wonderful, mystical, magical place and the intoxicating surrealistic landscape of this deeply shadowed chasm between majestic mountain ridges.

But what then? The scariest part of letting go of the known is the going on to the unknown. The known had been enchanting; there was nothing enchanting about my days now. They were somber and gray, filled with mundane tasks. I was still answering letters, writing to old friends and acquaintances who had not heard of the girls' deaths. Every day the mailman brought another pile of cards. The reading of those cards brought tears. Each little note, especially those that were a tribute to some aspects of one or both of the girls' lives, allowed a fresh release, a new comfort, and sometimes a bit of information about their lives. The navy gave our address to whoever wished to contact us. Dani's friends sent copies of photos they had of her; Roy's mom sent a newspaper article with a photo of Dani giving a speech before a large crowd of navy women. I didn't even know she had given that speech. She looked so competent and controlled as she stood at the podium dressed in her whites. I found the speech notes in her scrapbook.

The scrapbooks. My daughters had chronicled their lives. It was all there. I would start my day's activities and be distracted by that pile of books. I would settle down to reading, touching things with the palm of my hand, marveling at these lovely people who were my children. The wonder of it all was that there was not one word critical of anyone in any of their writings, not even of their parents. In one of Dawn's journals, I found an entry for the day on which I tried to convince her to give up her high school affair with a married teacher. We were so devastated by her entrapment. The man was a predator who had used Dawn's innocence and vulnerability and social incompetence to trap her. I had talked for hours, sometimes calmly, sometimes ranting. I had tried every tack to force her to see the situation for what it was. Afterward, I cried. I was certain that the child must hate me. The entry simply stated that we had talked for a long time, that her mother cared for her and was only trying to help her. I cried again. How could that little girl be so stupid as to have fallen for that jerk's ploys and so wise as to understand her mother's awkward attempts to thwart him?

Long ago I heard a story about the death of a young girl. Her parents were members of an ethnic group that had brought with it to this country the custom of saying good-bye to the possessions of the dead, especially when the dead one was young. A young friend was chosen and given the duty of informing the possessions that their friend was gone. I remembered this story; I would perform this duty for my daughters. Dawn's clothes had already been sorted. We did that at her apartment the same day we sorted Dani's clothes. I'm certain that Dawn's roommate was shocked at what appeared to be callous behavior. We held up each item, asked who wanted it, and then threw it into the proper pile. Before the others got there that morning, I went into Dawn's room and just stood there and looked at each little thing, thought about her placing it there, and remembered her attachment to each of her possessions. I opened the top drawer. Socks. Neatly folded in half and filed in rows. And a compact. Just like Dani's compact. I opened it to see if it had a mirror and powder. It did not; it contained a diaphragm. A sharp intake of breath and then laughter, peals of laughter. That other empty compact in Dani's purse was now explained.

I heard Debra at the door and ran to get her and show her the compact. The roommate overheard and came over to us; he said, "Do you mean that that girl went into eternity with that thing in her?" I don't know. Do you supposed the people who did the autopsy removed it? Or the people at the mortuary? Or is that piece of rubber rotting in a casket in a

74

grave on a hillside overlooking a valley that ends at nearby mountains?

We finished sorting all the clothes in the room. The roommate brought in boxes of T-shirts from his room. There hadn't been space in Dawn's room for them. She purchased a T-shirt wherever she went. She used to laugh until she cried about the one she bought in Paris from a girl about her own age who spoke no English. Since Dawn spoke no French, they effected the whole transaction in sign language and got so tickled at themselves that they were both convulsed with laughter. The shirts were stored like an intact collection. She didn't wear them. Neither did we. We took the entire collection to the Salvation Army. I hope the person who buys that shirt from Paris senses the happiness and silliness it represents.

The drawers and closets were all empty when I packed the apartment a few weeks later. The clothes were integrated into other wardrobes, but the bed was still made up. I had to unmake that bed. I had to move the clock from where she had reached out to turn off the alarm. I took down the ironing board. I removed the diplomas and family pictures from the walls. I packed her toiletries. Her hair dryer. Her toothbrush and toothpaste. The bubble bath. As I packed, I explained to each item that she was gone; I said good-bye for her to each article. Richard works for my husband; he offered to help me. He carried things to the truck—one load to the Salvation Army, one to the storage unit, and one to my house. My grandson had a fever that day and couldn't go to day care. He played on the floor while I worked. Finally, I sat in the rocking chair, the last piece of furniture in the apartment, and rocked him. I did not cry. Sometimes it hurts too much to cry.

Roy's family was having trouble. Gloria called often; his cousins and aunts and sisters called or wrote, asking for comfort. They hadn't seen him since last August. Only a box of ashes had come home. They weren't accepting his death. One day Gloria called and asked if Danny, Roy's brother, could come out and stay with us. He would ride his motorcycle across the United States and come visit us. I told her that of course Danny could come, of course he was welcome. He could sleep on the same couch his brother had slept on, but his brother was not here. His brother was dead. She turned from the phone and relayed the message to Danny. "She says Roy is not there; Roy is dead." Danny didn't come. We were having trouble, too. We needed to know more about the girls' death. We needed the details. Did they hurt? Was anyone conscious? Did they say anything? Debra investigated. She talked to the ambulance driver and the person who picked Dawn up off the pavement where witnesses to the accident had placed her. A very nice woman told Deb that she must think of Dawn and Dani as having died together. "I picked Dawn's head up in cardboard. She never knew anything about that wreck. Your two sisters died together." But what about all that stuff listed on the bill from the emergency room? The oxygen? The cut-downs? The attempts to restart her heart? The tracheotomy? "We have to do that. If we didn't try, we could be sued." Pete and I badgered the state police for the accident report. We couldn't let go of it until we knew every detail.

I needed to tell everybody. I am sure I embarrassed and discomfited many of the people I managed to tell. I took Dawn's phone back to the phone company. I couldn't just turn it in. I had to tell the clerk that my daughter had died, that this had been her phone, and that I was returning it for credit to her account. I bought brass cleaner at a kitchen shop. I had to tell the clerk that it was to polish the brass collection of my recently deceased daughter. I went to the storage unit where the navy had stored Dani's household goods. To open

76

the crate, I had to get special permission from Edwards Air Force Base, which is in charge of all navy storage in this part of the state. When everything was arranged, the moving and storage company assigned a fat, kind, and sensitive fellow to help me open and sort and move things. We worked together all day, uncrating, unwrapping, sorting into piles, rewrapping, relabeling, and repacking. Dani collected puzzles. She had boxes and boxes of puzzles. I gave them to my sensitive new friend. Somehow I could not become a repository for their collections. Some of Roy's things were included with Dani's shipment. These things were returned to military storage for shipment to his mother. Dani's kitchen things were repacked for storage until the house in North Carolina was built on the property Dani and I had picked out together. Her bed, her couch, and her sewing machine will go to North Carolina someday. Her good desk and chair and her armoir were integrated into our guest room, with Dawn's twin beds. The girls' perfumes, their framed photographs, are also on display there. Dani's flight suit and helmet went into storage alongside her father's Korean War uniforms. They were going to dress up in their uniforms on Veterans Day; they both had red, white, and blue corpuscles. It was a grueling day. As with Dawn's things, some of it was pure junk and I junked it. Some were family treasures and I kept them. Some were the girls' treasures and I kept some and gave some away. I went to the office of the moving company to ask a question and stayed to tell them the whole story of the girls' deaths and the funeral. I imagined that they wanted to hear it; I knew that I needed to tell it. I gave myself permission to keep telling it to any hapless victim I could find until I no longer needed to talk about it. That day finally did come. Finally, I was no longer defined by their deaths. I was me again—a different me, but not just the mother of two dead girls. Just me.

One Sunday morning I awoke knowing that we must

77

move. I found an ad in the Sunday paper, Pete and I went to see the house, and moved in the next week. It was a much larger house with a pool and a yard that needed lots of work. The move took us away from the hearth that Dawn sat on while she allowed me my glimpse of eternity, from the flower beds that Dani and I prepared for the wrong occasion, from the entry hall where Dawn stood two weeks after she died. Now there was room to fully integrate their furniture with ours. In this house, everything had always been exactly where it was now. There was no before and after the girls' deaths. We moved Dawn's couch to Pete's new office and placed her oak drafting table along the wall near his desk. Over it, we hung her hard hat and her diplomas. And some watercolors she had done. I found her sketch pad and framed everything in it. She would have laughed at me and snatched the drawings away, but they were the product of her talent and they are my treasures. What's left of her collection of storage tins sits on top of my refrigerator; I gave many to her friends. Dani's cannisters and storage jars are on a shelf in my kitchen, and the girls' kitchen witches, which they gave to each other, hang one over the other from my kitchen ceiling.

The yard needed hours of my time. The pool provided exercise to end depression. All summer long, I transplanted, planted, weeded, spaded, and created a beautiful garden where there had been neglect and sterile soil. When I found worms working the soil, I knew I had succeeded in bringing life to a dead place. As I worked, I healed. We all healed in the summer sunshine.

While I worked in the sun, physically busy, my mind was also digging and reorganizing. Something good had to come out of this; I had to learn and grow. I did not consciously plan to benefit emotionally or spiritually or mentally from the deaths of my daughters but that part of my brain that made accessible a glimpse of the borders of the place, which had arranged for me to have my life organized in such a way that I was free to join Dani for a trip and available to mediate the jostling for position that must occur when a family is reunited after a long separation, that part of me now worked to make a positive learning experience of each painful negative. I have never in my life really understood neurosis. When I was going to be tested on Freud's theories, I would rememorize the textbook definition of *neurosis* and then promptly forget it after the test. As I dug and weeded, I thought about Ruie and Milford and the lifetime of gamesmanship that has had such a deleterious effect on their children. I wondered that such good people could become so involved in destructive behavior. As I rocked back on my heels to rest at the edge of a flower bed, I was suddenly looking into my own brain. This was not a white and gray view of the cortex and caudate nucleus and cerebellum and other physical structures in the brain; this was a view of a schematic design of the functioning of my own brain. There were no words, no names or descriptions of what I was seeing. I was seeing walled off, secret territory in which were hidden the irrational fears of childhood. I saw how my mind worked to protect me from things that did not now exist and probably never existed in any real sense. I was designing whole behavior patterns and even life-styles around the protection of a part of me demanded by threats that were recorded without words, without labels, before language, in infancy and early childhood. I was shaken by the impenetrability of these defenses, by the inability of reason to act on that which is without words. Logic and reason are part of language, and these fears were before language. I sat for a timeless period and stared into this schematic design of my own brain. Now I knew neurosis; it is mine and it is a noun, a verb, and an adjective.

And while I worked in the sun, I waited. We were aware that the California Highway Patrol was preparing a report of their investigation of the accident. We knew that there were many color and black-and-white photos of the wreck and that the exact descriptions of the crash and the results of the crash were in that report. We heckled them from time to time, trying to induce them to hurry that report to us. Since it is possible to sue the state for the condition of the highway and their culpability in allowing the road to remain in that dangerous condition, the state was taking its time and doing a very thorough investigation. They were also repairing the highway. I knew that I was actively waiting for that report, but I was awaiting more than a typewritten report; I did not know what it was I awaited. Then the report was in the mailbox. I ran to a bench in the backyard and began to read:

Witness #2 related the following:

I was eastbound on Main Street approaching 12th Street. The light was green for me; as I started to enter the intersection I observed a large white car enter the intersection against the red light from southbound 12th Street to eastbound Main. The large white car was weaving left and right all over the road. It looked like the driver was drunk. His speed was about 25 miles per hour. The way he was seated, he looked very short. . . . As I proceeded eastbound on SR-126 there were now five vehicles between the large white car and my own. The white car was about 500 feet ahead' of me. We all went out of town at 35 to 40 miles per hour. As I approached the Linville Little Red Barn, which is a flower shop just west of Orcutt Road on the south side of the highway, I saw a large cloud of dust which I drove through. Just east of Orcutt Road the traffic stopped ahead of me. As I approached the accident scene I saw a large vehicle facing eastbound in the westbound traffic lane.

Witness #1 related the following:

I was westbound on SR-126 heading toward Santa Paula at about 50 miles per hour. I was following the Chevrolet and had been for several miles. He was about 150 feet in front of me. I didn't see any headlights coming in our direction but saw the rear of the Chevrolet go up in the air and back down again. I didn't see or hear anything else.

There was no evidence of evasive action on the part of either driver. The cars hit; the occupants and contents were thrown forward, demolishing the dashboards; the cars came to rest. And my children were dead or dying. And it was silent. There in the dark and the dust, it was silent. The witness didn't hear or see anything else.

And they were still dead. I was astonished to discover that some part of my brain was carefully guarding itself from the knowledge that they were dead by believing that the accident report when it finally came would reveal that this was all a mistake, that they were still alive. Now I was devoid of hope.

I have always been entranced by Aeschylus and the image he creates in *The Eumenides* of Athena making a deal with the Furies. They had been chasing down poor old Orestes for killing his mother Clytemnestra, a crime against primitive society. Athena saw that society must change, that this primitive vengeance must be replaced with law and civilization. She began to reason with these ancient goddesses; they responded:

Gods of the younger generation, you have ridden down the laws of the elder time, torn them out of my hands.

Athena quieted them with a promise:

In a complete honesty I promise you a place of your own, deep hidden under ground that is yours by right where you shall sit on shining chairs beside the hearth to accept devotions offered by your citizens.

They struggle on, the goddesses of the past bemoaning their lost position and Athena quieting them and explaining to them their new place in the order of things. At last, they acquiesce and put a spell upon the land:

> That the sun's bright magnificence shall break out
> wave on wave of all the happiness life can give,
> across the land.

Athena's last instructions to the old hags as they enter their new abode beneath the city and as Athena departs are to:

> hold off what might hurt the land; pour in the city's
> advantage, success in the end.

And the Furies promise the citizens of this city that "Life will give you no regrets." To me, those Furies clearly represent the unconscious or subconscious mind, buried beneath the conscious ego and superconscious superego. When first I read *The Eumenides*, I knew that Freud had read it, too, and built these ancient tales into his theories. In the healthy mind, the subconscious protects, defends, and blesses, but it does it in a primitive way, without communication in words with the conscious mind. I had been dimly aware that there was a part of me that did not yet believe that my daughters were dead; I had tried to communicate with that part but I knew that I did not succeed.

Now, as I read that report and listened to witnesses describe the soundless deaths of my children, those ancient goddesses writhed and screamed and wailed. They had failed to protect; their prayer for the blessing of the happiness life can give, for a life that gives no regrets, had not been answered. They could no longer hold off what might hurt the land. They were like psychotic old hags, glaring out of tortured eyes, made wild and ugly by rage and fear and pain. The order of things was not as it should be; they were threatened once again. At last, they needed to hear me. At last, all the parts of my mind were able to work together; the part of the brain that is Athena once again struggled with them, promised them, quieted them. And once again they were at peace, satisfied that they were doing their duty and that the city was safe. Now I could really say good-bye to the lives of my daughters. With my whole self, I could say good-bye. Without regret, dear Furies, I believed they were gone—and the city was still safe.

CHAPTER SIX

We didn't make many trips to the cemetery. In the first few weeks, we went out several times a week. We took our little grandson and his mama and we sat on the edge of the graves and peered down through the dirt at those wooden boxes still glowing with captured sunlight. The flowers still seemed visible, perched on the top of each casket. The baby played and rolled and tumbled on the graves; we sat carefully beside them. The headstones had not yet been delivered. We watched the ground settle and the grass begin to grow again after having been disturbed.

Dani's birthday was in April. She always loved daisies. There is a song about a man who loved a girl in his village and promised to bring her a daisy a day for each day of their lives. Dani always asked for that song to be played and sung at her birthday celebrations; the little band at the country club learned it in self-defense. On her twenty-sixth birthday, I ordered a huge bouquet of white daisies with yellow centers and took them to her grave. I sat beside the grave and sang to her. The song ends with the death of the woman in old age and the old man still walking to the cemetery on the hill, bringing her a daisy a day. I went alone to the grave that day; so did Pete. He often did that. He said that he would be driving along, headed toward the job or the office and would suddenly turn his car toward the cemetery and then would sit in the sun and watch the valley below and visit with his daughters. Darcy drove out there from school; Debra reported that she sometimes drove out to sit and be with them. As the summer wore on, we went less and less often. The headstones arrived. It was very difficult to see their names there. I had always been so proud of their names: Dani Lynn and Dawn Marie. Now I didn't like to see those names there on the ground, surrounded by grass that needed to be weeded and fertilized.

We learned to fly. Pete said we needed something to talk about other than death. We needed to have an interest that would demand our time and attention. Although I had never been up in a small plane and had never wanted to be, we began to take flying lessons. We went to ground school one night a week. We took the written test and passed it. We did our required cross-country flights. We met people who didn't know us when we had four daughters and who only talked about flying. They would never need to endure the litany of the deaths.

I cried sometimes. Pete did not. I asked him if he were free to cry and he said, "Not really." I said that I was sorry. It is so much harder for men who are not allowed to cry. Darcy wrote poems and talked to her friends, and she tried to write a song about her sisters. Debra got married; Dennis beat out the other two suitors and there was a small wedding in our backyard. The pastor who assisted at the funeral performed this ceremony for us, too. Debra's mourning became a private thing, shared with her new husband. We sat around the pool in the hot sun and remembered Dani and Dawn. We were not selective; we remembered the ribald and the raunchy just as fondly as we remembered the sweet and the sacred.

We remembered Dawn's childhood fear of passing a car. She could be completely relaxed in the back seat, but when her father pulled out to pass the car in front, she would jump to her feet, stare down the road, tense, and if it took long enough to get back into our own lane, she would scream shrilly until all perceived danger had passed. Her fear of a head-on collision seemed completely irrational then, but now our memory of a terrified little child holding the back of the driver's seat and screaming made us ask some questions for which there are no real answers.

The photograph albums and scrapbooks stretch across the bottom shelf of a fourteen-foot-wide bookcase. Both of the brunettes had had photo albums which had been carefully maintained since the third or fourth grade. The haphazard results of their first attempts at photography are preserved, most of them blurry and either too far away from or too close to their subjects. And most of their subject matter was each other. They posed for each other for hours at a time over a period of ten years. They would hang a sheet on the wall to make a backdrop and then dress up in lingerie or pajamas or ski clothes or other people's formal clothes. They took these photo sessions very seriously; although some of the pictures are of little girls making faces, most are of young beauties pretending to model professionally. They are stilted, amateurish, and striking. There are photos of their classmates, their boyfriends, their family, and of each other. Horse shows, boat trips, ski trips, summer camps, slumber parties, birthdays, Christmas, and their baby sister—born when Dawn was seven years old—are interspersed with the bedroom modeling sessions.

The photo of Dawn's seventh birthday bicycle is there, but the one taken a few days later when she went over the handlebars of that bike and lost her permanent front tooth in the gravel in front of the house is missing. It was taken out once too often to show and tell at school. Dani took it to school the next day after the accident and reported to a gleeful Dawn that the teacher shuddered when she saw that bloody little face lying on a pillow that was protected with a bloody blue towel. The photo is gone, but there is a space where it was; in my memory the photo is still carefully preserved.

Dawn was so intelligent that she made herself miserable. She taught herself to read when she was four years old. Dani says that she taught her, but Dani had a reading handicap and, at five years old, didn't know much more about reading than the letters of the alphabet. Dawn was intense, observed, asked detailed questions, and remembered everything she was told and that she observed. She was quiet, but her big brown eyes never stopped looking and seeing. She seemed wise when she viewed the behavior of others but totally unaware of her own intense overreaction to stimuli. She was born with a nervous system disorder that caused her to have problems controlling her bladder and bowels. She wet the bed until she was seven; she also sucked her thumb until she was seven. She could read, but she couldn't control her bladder. She was so skinny that my sister-in-law accused me of keeping her wrapped in swaddling blankets for the first year of her life. Her interest in food was purely functional; she knew when she was hungry and when she was full and would eat nothing after she felt full. She was not very well coordinated, so looked like a pretty little Ichabod Crane until she reached her teens.

All the girls had studied ballet from the time they were about four years old. There are framed photographs on the wall in the guest room of little girls in tutus and makeup, smiling proudly. Dawn is the skinny one who looks like her arms and legs are not connected to a controlling motor center from the elbow and knee down. She always knew the dance perfectly; she simply could not seem to align her body and control her big feet and hands. Her teacher would look at me defensively when Dawn danced. Finally, one day, I told her that I knew that it wasn't her fault, that Dawn just did not seem to be connected to her feet and hands, that Dawn was happy and completely unaware of her lack of grace and line, therefore we would just tough is out. Dawn once broke her finger falling *up* the stairs. She got a concussion falling off the fender of the truck parked in the garage. She could not ride a horse; she did wrap her long legs around the stomach of our pony and manage to stay on, but a combination of fear and awkwardness put equitation far beyond her ken.

Dawn never could express her emotional needs directly, but she was a master of the indirect statement. When she was four, she had a closet with a low rod and little hangers. She was supposed to hang up her coat when she came in. I would check to see if she had done as she was told. The coat would be nowhere in sight—not in the closet, not on the floor, not on or under the bed. Then I would notice the outline of her coat under the bedspread. She had carefully pulled back the spread, laid her coat flat on her bed, and covered it with the smoothed bedspread. All of this effort was performed only three feet from the coat hanger on the low rod in the closet. I spanked her. She would repeat the performance the next day. Finally, in desperation, I asked the family physician what he thought was going on. He said she needed more attention and was assuring herself that she would get it, even though the attention she got was a spanking. I was puzzled, dumbfounded, amazed. Why would a little four-year-old girl set herself up to get spanked when she could have been praised with less effort? I increased the amount of time and attention she received and the behavior stopped, but I never really understood.

Her emotions were never sheathed. She sat one night on the couch beside her daddy. She reached up her long, skinny arm and put it around him and said, "Isn't it glad to be married?" Her daddy instinctively realized that Dawn meant her marriage to him, and he jumped up off of that couch and paced around in front of the poor, bony little girl who was in love with her daddy and couldn't conceal it. When she was lost in the supermarket (and she was lost in the supermarket almost every time we went shopping because she would stop to read the cereal boxes and get left behind), she would panic and scream so loud that everyone in the store looked as if they were under attack. I would come running to the sound of the scream and there she would be, by the cereal boxes, with her jaw unhinged and the most horrible air-raid siren coming out of that little body. Although she got her bottom swatted for making such a scene, she never learned to look for us before she started screaming. There was never a time lag between feeling the emotion and acting on it. Yet she was tolerant of the emotional hang-ups and aberrant behavior of others. She would simply observe. She remembered everything I ever did as a parent, but without blaming me for those things I really didn't want anyone to remember, least of all me. They just were; she just was.

Dani was cuddly and pretty and loving, but so intensely loving that one shied from the weight of her love. She was determined and courageous and not nearly so well coordinated physically as she thought she was. She always told you how well she did at something athletic, but if you believed her you were in for a surprise when she actually performed for you. She loved to wear the costume of a cheerleader or a saddle-seat rider or a dancer and she would practice diligently at the skills involved, but it never really paid off. She was always stiff and stilted. She could not sit a Western saddle; her excitement at being in a show ring would cause her to tense her muscles and pull herself to a standing position in the stirrups. She won several trophies at showmanship because she could stand rigid and alert for hours, smiling sweetly at the judge. She did win one first place trophy at junior saddle seat equitation, but I was always pretty sure the trainer had bribed the judge. It didn't matter, though; she cherished that silver tray for the rest of her life.

She loved babies. She baby-sat whenever she got a chance.

There is a photo of her holding Dawn when Dani was about two years old and Dawn about four months. Dawn looks a little uncomfortable, but Dani is glowing. She pestered me for that baby from the time she could talk; she was to do that again when Darcy was on the way. I actually had to fight Dani to get to have the baby in my room at night. When she died, her billfold was full of pictures of other people's babies. Roy called her in the last week of her life to discuss with her the way she spoiled her dogs. Dani had three dogs of her own in her life, one cocker and two Labs. All three were undisciplined, obnoxious, and destructive. Dani did nothing to correct their behavior. Roy knew those last two dogs and was appalled at Dani's unwillingness to discipline them. During that last weekend at our house, we teased Dani about the way she spoiled her dogs and warned her that her children would have to have more discipline than she had been able to muster for her dogs. Roy had been thinking about that. He called to talk about the fact that he would be out on a ship for six months at a time; he wanted a promise that he would not come home to undisciplined, spoiled little brats. Dani assured him that she only spoiled dogs, that she was very good with children. And she was. She wanted six; she had none.

Dani could always fall asleep anywhere. When she was a toddler, she disappeared one afternoon. I looked for her all over the new subdivision in which we lived. I organized the neighbors and we extended the search to nearby open fields and woods. On the lot next to us was an unfinished house, sided but with no fireplace in the opening and bare deck still exposed between open framed walls. I think it was my dog that led me into that fireplace opening. There was little Dani, fanny up in the air, cheek down on that rough subfloor, sound asleep. Whenever she was tired, she simply fell asleep. Dawn, on the other hand, needed all her props and complete silence to go to sleep. She sucked her thumb until she was seven, and she had a *suvy*. I think she combined *soft* and *fluffy* to get *suvy*, but a *suvy* was the satin on the edge of a blanket, or her slip, or the silky tag on a stuffed animal. She would get her *suvy* just so, and then her thumb went into her mouth and she would drift off to sleep. As she grew older, she gave up the thumb and the *suvy* and replaced them with complete silence and complete darkness, neither of which was attainable in college dorms or the dormitory-like existence with three sisters. She would thrash around in the bed and yell at the person who violated her silence and darkness. She was not a nice person when she was trying to go to sleep.

Dani had her tonsils out when she was only two. They were so large that the physician brought them out of the operating room for me to see. I was not impressed, never having seen any tonsils at all and therefore being unable to make a comparison. They had blocked her nasal passages so that she had been unable to chew with her mouth closed and had settled for sucking her food and rubbing it on the roof of her mouth with her tongue. That tongue habit led to braces when she was about eleven. She had to wear the headgear that rubbed a bald spot in her hair, but she was religious about it, even about the rubber band that held her tongue down. Dawn had braces, too. Her thumb had moved her front teeth. Because of the accident with her bicycle, she wore them twice in her life: once when she was ten or eleven and again in her junior and senior year of high school. The girls never resented the braces, never did the silly stuff with the closed lip smile that some girls do. They considered the braces a privilege and often talked about their expensive smiles.

Both of the girls could sew; both owned sewing machines and operated them with skill. Technically, their products were perfect; however, Dawn's were also beautiful. Dani's were frumpy. She chose the wrong fabric and the wrong pattern. Nobody wanted her to wear the things she had made for herself. Dawn's garments were elegant; she had to tell you that she had made them or you would not guess. I was amazed at some of the scraps I found in her scrap bag; I really had not known that some of those garments were homemade. But Dani did make some things that are treasures. The overalls she embroidered for Darcy were clever and well executed. There was a Big-Mac, complete with all the ingredients plainly visible; there was a school emblem; there were flowers; there was a horse. From top to bottom, front and back, those overalls were covered with originals designs and extravagant color. And there was the tree skirt for the Christmas tree; it is beautifully made. And the ten-foot-long muffler she crocheted for Darcy with the name of the school team in block letters from one end to the other. It was a real hit at school games. Both girls were artists with thread and fabric; Dani just lacked taste when it came to her own clothes.

Both of them played with math like it was a puzzle or a game. They wanted a supergraphic on the wall of their bedroom. In a matter of a few minutes, they whipped out their pocket calculators and, as they explained to me later, used a bit of algebra and had the supergraphic perfectly proportioned to the cathedral ceiling and the size of the room. I was awe-struck. Dani once played the part of an absent-minded professor at our annual Thanksgiving talent show. Her lecture: "Give me an equation. Just any equation. Your favorite quadratic equation will do." No one *had* a favorite quadratic equation, so she produced one. It never occurred to her that not everyone in that room could even remember what a quadratic equation was; she thought we were just being shy.

Dawn's IQ was 160. She scored the lowest ever scored at the testing center on the category test, which tests the ability to realize the concept behind a group of examples. In two categories, Dawn didn't even miss the one usually required to test the concept. She just knew. Dani's IQ was high, but not that high. She had the reading disability that slowed the acquisition of information. She could not spell, because she did not really remember how the word looked from one time to the next. I once got a letter from her that seemed somehow strange. In a postscript, she asked: "Does this letter seem different to you, Mom? I looked up almost every word. There is not one misspelled word in the whole letter." She was wrong; there were a couple, but nothing like her usual quasiphonetic spelling. When she got the job as career counselor in the navy, she had to write reports. In an act of self-discipline and will, she forced herself to know when she did not know. She would make lists of each word she had misspelled and memorize the correct spelling from her spelling list.

Dani was doggedly determined. She was not talented, but she was determined. She did not know she was a winner; she always assumed she was in a losing position and then ducked her head, gritted her teeth, and concentrated her effort in order to improve her position. She took every remedial reading class available to her in school. She found a remedial reading specialist who lived in our neighborhood and who would trade baby-sitting for tutoring. Every summer, Dani peddled her bike over there twice a week, once to baby-sit and once to have a tutoring session. She didn't want to lose what little skill she had over the summer months. Her father had played the trumpet in high school. He still had his trumpet, all bent up and not too shiny. Dani wanted to be like her father, so she learned to play the trumpet. She never had formal individual lessons; she studied with the instructor of the school band, all through junior and senior high school. She played with the junior symphony, but she only played first chair one week and then got challenged and moved to second chair. When there were three trumpets, she was third chair. But she played and she practiced and she could say she played in the high school band and in the junior symphony. She studied ballet from age five until she was a senior in high school. She was never very good, but she did get to advance to toe shoes and she did try out for every performance and event available to her. She danced with the ballet class when they performed *The Nutcracker* for the symphony's annual Christmas concert. She wasn't wonderful, but she knew the steps and performed them correctly, and she loved it. She was dressed as a dancer, wearing toe shoes, and onstage. And she did it without having any talent; she had determination.

But both girls were losers when it came to the men in their lives. There was a rule in our house that you could not double-date until you were fifteen and you could not single-date until your sixteenth birthday. Both girls waited with great anticipation for their fifteenth birthdays. Nothing happened. No one asked them out. Now, they had had little boyfriends in the second grade and in the sixth grade, boys who gave them little gifts and sent them notes. Dani never forgave me for making her give back a necklace that one of them had given her. She was right; it was unforgivable. I was enforcing rules that no longer existed, except in the mind of my mother: girls do not accept jewelry from boys other than their fiancés. Little boys on bicycles had cluttered our driveway when the girls were too young to date; then they were fifteen and there were no boys. They waited. They turned sixteen. Nothing happened. When Dawn turned sixteen, there was a nice boy who took her out once or twice and then moved away. Obviously, the girls were doing something wrong. They had no brothers; they did not know how to behave around boys, especially boys who were eligible as romantic interests. They were self-conscious and awkward and came on much too strong. Dani had to import her date for the junior prom from Portland. He was an ugly little duckling and she was embarrassed, but it was a way to wear a formal and go to the prom. Her date for her senior prom was an Italian boy who was very much in love with himself. He wasn't very tall; Dani was short; therefore, she made a good date. She was also quiet; he could do all the talking—about himself. She enjoyed the prom, but she dropped him soon after. Desperate as she was, she wasn't going to put up with him. In college, she fell in love with a young man who was bothered by the fact that she wasn't Catholic. She brought him home for the Symphony Ball. He was pleasant, good-looking, and intelligent. They dated for all of their freshman year. He wrote to her from home during the summer: he had decided to become a priest. They vowed to remain friends. They did, until he married his girl-next-door. Then Dani entered a period of depression. Her jobs were not the kind that allowed her to meet the man of her dreams. She did date the head cook a couple of times, but he stood her up more often than he showed up. She dated the brother of a friend of ours, but he would show up at her house in grubby blue jeans, hair uncut, face unshaved, and order her to change into something more glamorous. She was not assertive; she did as he said for a month or two. Finally, she had her fill. She ordered him out of her house; she told him that he had no right to come in there all grubby and criticize how she looked and dressed. She met an older man while waiting tables. She dropped him. An old friend from Portland, that boy who came up to take her to the prom, moved in with her for a week. She asked him to leave. And all the time, she told herself that Mr. Right was out there somewhere, that he would make her happy.

She waited to be a bride. She believed that all her loneliness would go away if she was married. I tried to convince her that marriage was a commitment between two people who could not imagine life apart and did not change who and what the two people were. If one was depressed before one married, one would probably be more depressed afterward, because of the disappointment that marriage had not taken away one's depression. She listened but she did not hear. I made the speech many times in the next three years.

Then Dani joined the navy. And she met Melvin. He was six feet, six inches tall and right out of the Louisiana swamps. He needed a mother; Dani needed someone to mother. They moved in together. They had lived together almost a year when we asked Dani to bring him home to meet her family. He had given her an engagement ring; she was planning the same wedding she had been planning all her life. The occasion was her grandfather's birthday party on the Oregon coast. Four generations of family would be there; we would spend a long weekend in a rented house on the beach. Melvin and Dani arrived while I was out of town; I joined them for dinner at my aunt's house. As I entered the room, six foot, six inches of little boy stood up. I looked at Dani; I saw her embarrassment and her disappointment. I tried to make the best of it. She was seeing him through her father's eyes and the eyes of her mother and sisters and she was ashamed of him. We all tried to ease her discomfort. We entertained him royally. He was impressed; he asked Pete for money to start a sporting goods business. He was ignored.

We drove to the coast, passing snow-covered Mount Hood. Melvin was angry that we did not make the four-hour side trip that would have taken him to the snow. He had never seen any snow. We had a seven-hour drive in two overloaded cars ahead of us. We opted not to add the four hours to that. He pouted. At the beach house, he refused to help with any chores and sulked because he had to sleep on a couch. Dani's grandfather took out the garbage after Melvin refused, for which act he incurred the wrath of the whole family, including Dani. Melvin's popularity, almost nonexistent when we first saw him, had vanished completely. Dani's birthday was just two days after her grandfather's. We had a bridal lingerie shower for her there by the fire in the beach house, with the surf pounding on one side and the lake rain-speckled on the other. She was enchanted with the satin and lace; Melvin was jealous. There was a black silk undershirt and shorts for him, but he wasn't impressed.

As they were preparing to leave for Florida, I happened to walk by the downstairs bathroom while they were getting dressed. Melvin had his arm around Dani's neck from behind and was choking her. He was angry like a bully is angry. He knew we didn't like him and that Dani had seen him through our eyes and didn't like him, either. He was hurting her. I said nothing. He stopped when he saw me watching. I waited. As soon as I knew that they were back in their house in Florida, I called Dani. I told her to get him out of that house and to do it now. I explained to her that his violence could only get worse as he compared himself to her and to the rest of the world and didn't measure up. He was trying very hard to bring her down to his level. By insulting her and by pouting and by teaching her to try to avoid physical violence, he was making every possible attempt to destroy the Dani that had attracted him in the first place. I told her that I would come to visit her in June and that he was to be out of there by then. I waited.

June came. Melvin was still there. I called her and told her that I did not need to visit her and would not if he was still in that house. I would skip Florida and go straight to North Carolina. She begged me to come. The night before I was to leave, she called and asked me to please come; she said that Melvin was out of the house. I went; Darcy came along. I also took along thirteen boxes of Dani's household goods, including her favorite stuffed animals. Melvin was indeed gone but his possessions were not. Obviously, Melvin was planning to move back in as soon as I left. We talked about it; I packed him up. We even sorted the photographs, giving him all the ones of him, including ones of him wearing Dani's

97

new bridal lingerie, which had been taken when they returned from our house. We made an attempt to deliver all his stuff to him on base, but couldn't find him in, so we moved everything into a buddy's garage. She returned the rings. He got the message. Dani and Darcy and I left town for our trip to visit relatives in North Carolina. When Dani returned to duty, Melvin made some forays into her house, which resulted in his arrest. Dani had her old determined spirit back, and she took every proper legal step. The navy helped. Her commanding officer called Melvin Jethro and congratulated her on getting him out of her life. I bought Dani some new clothes and talked her into wearing make-up every day. She claimed she didn't have time, so we simplified the procedure and made it as much a part of her routine as brushing her teeth and combing her hair. We talked about self-esteem and looking as good as she could to convince others and herself of her personal worth. It worked. Dani began to blossom. She advanced her rank; she met people she had worked with for two years who hadn't noticed her before. She grew up. She valued herself and her abilities. She took college math courses and got A's. She joined the Big Sister program. And Roy discovered her. When she finally quit looking for him, there he was.

Pete is jealous of the men his daughters bring home. He likes being the big bull seal on the beach and does not willingly and gracefully allow his position with his daughters to be challenged by their young swains. He usually pointedly ignores them or gets very busy in another part of the house when they are about. Roy would not tolerate that. He would get right up in Pete's face and say, "Mr. White, what do you think about . . . ?" He was so polite and so charming and genuinely sweet that Pete had no recourse. He had to talk to him. On that long weekend when Dani and Roy arrived from Florida, Roy wanted to show Pete his survival suit. It was a complex garment, used for jumping from an helicopter into the ocean to rescue seamen. He brought it all in from his car and gave a demonstration, using the tiled entry area as his platform. He was so excited about the suit and the training it represented that he was contagious. Pete couldn't resist him and his enthusiasm. He was soon off of his seat on the couch and over by Roy, inspecting the knives and flashlights and pockets and zippers of that garment. Roy just smiled his way right past all those defenses against boys who weren't really good enough for Pete's daughters. Roy was good enough; he was even good enough to convince Pete.

Roy had two sisters; our daughters had no brothers. The girls had always been a bit self-conscious when there was a boy in the house. They weren't quite certain that boys were of the same species as girls. Roy smiled his way past the stiffness and awkwardness; he was relaxed and loving. He had strong opinions, but he was so gentle in expressing them that he raised no hackles. He and I went for a bike ride with Dani. We visited as we rode along. He told me that he had a friend from his hometown in Michigan who was living near San Diego. He was genuinely concerned about his friend because he was a model. Roy thought that might indicate that he was a homosexual. I teased Roy unmercifully about his bias against male models and homosexuals. He laughed, but he did not allow my teasing to alter his strongly held opinion that his friend might be lost to him because of homosexuality, due to the fact that he was a model. Roy was an altar boy who had never lost his faith. His Bible was heavily underlined; his morals were old-fashioned and unquestioned. And he loved Dani wholly, proudly. He waited awhile after Melvin left her life, because he didn't approve of Melvin or the fact that they had lived together. But then he was there for her—for the rest of her life.

But before Roy and after Melvin, Dani's wedding dress

99

arrived. It was beautiful. She put it on and walked around the house in it. She called her neighbor and asked her to come over and take a picture of her in that dress. I found the picture in her album after she died. She is standing in her kitchen, in front of her back door. Her bulletin board, with its wall phone surrounded by an ornamental tape and its list of phone numbers, the memo pad, the calendar, and an envelope pinned to it, is beside her. The corner of her sewing machine cover is visible. Dani is smiling; her hands are clenched into fists like a small child's when it is excited. Her dark hair and dancing eyes capture one's attention but then one must look at the soft chiffon Gibson girl sleeves and the lace-covered bosom. The tiara is nowhere in sight. She didn't wear it when she was buried, either. As I looked at the picture, I remembered lecturing her about the dangerous attitude that she could be a Barbie doll dressed in her bridal gown and could insert just any Ken doll dressed in his wedding clothes and live happily ever after. I don't think she heard me; Dani never stopped wanting to be a bride.

Dawn did not fare any better than Dani. In her junior year of high school, with Dani's cooperation, she began an affair with one of her teachers. The girls had been baby-sitting for him and his wife. I began to be bothered when the wife showed up at the stable to ride the horses. I didn't understand why adults were choosing children as their peers and literally coming over to play, in the pool, on the tennis court, and at the stable. I pumped Dani, but got nowhere. Then Dawn told us that she was going steady with a football jock, one of the most popular boys in her senior class. We relaxed our vigilance, although we did not allow the teacher and his wife to come over to play anymore. Dawn went to her senior prom with the jock. One day, near the end of the school year, I dropped by campus looking for Dawn. A student told me that the teacher and Dawn had left campus together. My intuition signaled danger. I watched Dawn as closely as I could that summer. She spent a lot of time with Dani at Dani's apartment. She went to Europe on the graduation present trip we give all our children. She worked. We spent lots of family time on the boat. Then, when Dawn went away to college, I got a letter. The letter claimed that she and the teacher had met at a school game and fallen in love, that he was separated from his wife and getting divorced and that made it okay. It asked for permission to date him from home on weekends and vacations. I knew immediately. I called Dani and came down so hard that she could muster no defense and had to tell me the whole story. I was able to fill in the blank spots from the information I had stored in my memory, from all the unanswered questions over the past two years. Then I called Dawn. I told her that I knew the truth and that I certainly would not give my permission for him to come to our house. I tried desperately to explain to her what kind of an adult preys on gullible students. I tried to force her to look at the marriage and the children in the home she was disrupting. She was unimpressed, as well she should be. She knew a lot more than I did about that home. I later discovered that the wife had been having an affair with the football jock and that they had used our home when we were away to tryst—she and the jock in our living room, her husband and my daughter in my bed.

I suffered for Dawn, but we never discussed it again. She was busy at school; he was in our hometown. I preferred to imagine that they weren't able to see each other. I was wrong. He drove to campus every weekend and picked her up; they spent the weekend in his apartment, and then he drove her back. He called her daily. She was isolated from her peers and was enjoying none of the weekend activities that are part of campus life. This went on for two years. At the Christmas holiday in her sophomore year, he took her on a skiing trip.

She skied too hard the first day and was sick the second. While she was ill, he made passes at every skirt, or female in ski pants, in the lodge. Dawn watched. When she got back home, she went back to school as if everything were normal. However, when he went back to work, she got a friend to drive her to his apartment. She had painted, furnished, and decorated that apartment. Many of the furnishings were theirs jointly or had been gifts from one to the other. She loaded it all up. He came home to a stripped apartment. She went back to school. He followed her. Her friends were aware of what was going on. When he arrived, they banded around her and would not allow him to be alone with her. He left town without Dawn Marie and without his possessions.

The rumor had started to spread around town. Darcy heard that the man was depressed because he had lost his girl friend, that his students were aware of his love life and were sympathizing with him. We waited, holding our breath. Dawn came home the next weekend. She walked into the living room, crossed the room with her long, awkward arms outspread, began to cry, and said, "Oh, Mama, why didn't I listen to you?"

"Because you had to learn it for yourself. If it's over, I'm happy."

Then the fun began for Dawn. Her friends gave her an intensive course in college extracurricular activities. She drank beer in all the proper places. They took great pride in their assumed responsibility for having rescued Dawn from the creep. We also tried to rescue other little girls from the creep, but we failed. We hired an attorney. He said it was too dangerous for us to pursue it, that the creep was waiting for us to sue so that he could countersue for defamation of character, as had recently been done in the state in a similar situation. We met with school board members and the superintendent of schools. The first promised action that never came, and the latter treated the matter as an old-fashioned rape trial: "If what you say is true . . ." We could prove it was true, but no one wanted to hear. We solved our dilemma by telling everyone in the community who would listen so that other parents would be aware of the danger. This course had mixed results. Some parents listened; some did not. He had several other little girl friends before he remarried and I quit keeping track of him.

Dawn never again had a boyfriend who claimed to be in love with her. She had lovers, but they were friends who also made love to her. She also had some male friends who loved her very dearly but who were neither romantically nor sexually interested in her. She pretended not to care, but she confided to her sister Debra that during the year 1984, she would find a husband. She wanted to be married. She wanted someone to love her *and* to be in love with her. She only lived one month and twenty-four days of 1984, but she would not have succeeded. The man she had chosen as her leading candidate was bisexual, if not homosexual, a fact she chose to deny. Dawn was lonely; she would have gone on being lonely for a long time. She had friends, good friends, loyal friends, but she had no lover and she yearned for one. Somehow, this girl who was a romantic at heart could not inspire romance in other hearts. Probably she was still throwing her arms around necks and chirping, "Isn't it glad to be married?" She was still so intense that she frightened them all into jumping up and pacing the floor.

Chapter Seven

As the girls matured, they seemed to gain physical prowess. Dani swam like a fish and earned a lifeguard card while in high school. She was lifeguard for the navy. We sat around the pool with her on one of our trips to Florida. She took the job very seriously, allowing no foolishness in the pool, and swam a mile a day to keep in shape for rescuing folks. She had a red and white swim suit, red terry-cloth cover-up and a white cap with a big bill; the cover-up said Life-guard on it. It would. Dani always liked to dress the part. She looked so efficient and cute and she actually had attained the skill level that she thought she had.

Before she went in the navy, Dani and her father took scuba lessons. While she didn't love swimming underwater to the next tank for her next breath of air, she mastered scuba diving. They went to Puget Sound for their graduation dive. Both she and her father were very upset at how disorganized the dive and the dive master were. They got separated from the other divers and spent a seasick hour bobbing on the top of rough waters, waiting to be discovered by their recalcitrant dive master. Both of them said, "Plan your dive and dive your plan! Hah!" Dani was often disgusted with other people's lack of organization and pride.

In the navy, Dani was in her element. She loved the uniforms and wore one whenever she could. She loved basic training, grooving on the marching in step and flag waving. No one loves basic training, but Dani did. When she got to her special school and was the only girl in an all-male unit, she was often left sitting on the sidelines. No one wanted her on their team. One day a team member got a cramp and couldn't do his part of the relay. She bounced up and down on the bench and begged to be sent in. The officer in charge finally did send her, saying, "This is your chance to show 'em, Dani." She showed 'em, all right. She raced down to the line, flopped to the ground, and did her sit-ups and push-ups with lightning speed, and raced back to the finish line while her competitor was still on the ground doing his push-ups. At the enlisted men's club later that afternoon, he mildly scolded her, "Dani, you embarrassed me." But she never got left on the bench again. She practiced so hard at the obstacle course that she beat the men's time. Physically, it had come together for Dani.

And for Dawn. She got the most-improved trophy for girls' track in her senior year of high school. She started to run off the track as well. We ran with her for the first few steps and then she simply floated off and left us. Her long legs seemed to eat up the ground effortlessly. She ran up to ten miles a day. In college, she signed up for ballroom dancing classes. We chuckled, remembering the gangly, angly little girl in the tutus with the drooping hands and buckled knees. But she was good! She could hardly wait for the annual Symphony Ball to bring her partner and show us how good they were. She took a ballet class. Darcy had fourteen years of ballet classes behind her and considered herself something of a judge of ability. She went to visit Dawn at college, watched the class, and grudgingly admitted that Dawn was good. Maturity brought coordination; Dawn had always had the patience and determination.

Darcy and Dawn were an interesting pair. Dawn had been the baby for seven years when Darcy came along. Dawn did not willingly give up her position as the baby of the family; she made up her mind to hate that baby and did for several years. No one noticed because Dani loved Darcy enough for all of the sisters. Because no one noticed, Dawn made it a point to tell Debra and Dani periodically how much she hated that baby. She didn't tell me, ever. Darcy, on the other hand, may have hated Dawn or may not have—no one would have noticed because Darcy was always so busy loving herself that it didn't matter much how she felt about other people. Whatever she felt for Dawn, she definitely respected her intelligence. She would allow no other person to teach her anything. Whatever information she was given, she checked it out with Dawn. Skinny, jittery, hyper Dawn would yell the answer. Darcy just took it. If she could only get reliable information at the top of Dawn's decibel range, then that was how she would get it. That arrangement continued until Dawn left for college, which coincided with the time that Darcy decided that no one else in the world knew anything, anyway—a position she carefully preserved until the end of her seventeenth year.

After Dawn went away to college, she began to play the role of the proper big sister away at college. She invited Darcy up to stay with her in the dorm. During that weekend, Mount Saint Helens blew her top and stranded them there for ten days. Dawn almost lost her mind, while Darcy played the part of the college-dorm girl to the hilt, charming the other girls on the floor and returning Dawn to her original position of hating that kid. She resorted to desperate measures and invented a way to get that kid out of that town, lava dust be hanged.

Dawn's portfolio is on the shelf with the other albums and scrapbooks. It is black wool and leather, very slim and elegant. She picked it out on a trip to Portland and her father bought it for her. Every architecture graduate must make a portfolio; it is what they use to present their work to prospective employers. One chooses a theme or motif; Dawn's is in grays and beige. She chose her best work, photographed it, and mounted it between plastic covers for each page. The watercolor she did of a snow-blanketed farm near campus and gave to us for Mother's Day and Father's Day is there. Design assignments are reproduced and reduced and mounted. The tent she designed and built is there, with Dawn standing beside it. She copied the Izod insignia and sewed it to the side of the tent; she also made herself a running suit from the tent material. Photographs of the motel and apartment complexes she designed for her father are there, along with miniaturized blueprints of each projects. Not many students had any work experience, so she made a whole section for these photos and plans. I remember how she fussed and worried over that portfolio, how she complained about the cost of reproducing her work, and how proudly she carried it with her to her one and only job interview.

As I pulled the portfolio from the shelf to look at it one more time before describing it, an oversized card fell out on the floor. The cover showed a pair of giant feet in tennis shoes, protruding from the bottom of a graduation gown. The card reads: "Congratulations, Graduate . . . on your tremendous feat!" Dani had written a note on the inside:

Dawn, I realized this is probably a "boy" graduation card, and I also realize graduation is suposed [sic] to be serious stuff. Please accept this card and my apology that goes with it 'cause I just couldn't resist.

As usual, the gift will be slightly after the fact. I am sending it with Darcy.

I do hope you get all you want out of life and whatever you were hoping for in these last five years. I know you'll do great at whatever job you apply your skills to. You are a very talented person and I know you'll do great.

Good luck and Have Fun,
Dani
P.S. Remember, no more summer vacation! (over)

On the back she had written in block letters:

THIS BIRTHDAY CARD WAS PRESENTED (BY
MAIL) TO MY YOUNGER SISTER DAWN MARIE
WHITE TO CONGRATULATE HER GRADUA-
TION FROM COLEGE [sic] IN MEMORANCE [sic]
OF A BIRTHDAY CARD SENT TO ME (FROM HER)
THAT READ SOMETHING TO THE TUNE OF:
Where have all the years gone . . . a little to the hips,
a little to the waist, and a little to the thighs.
I love you, Dawn. Good luck!
Dani

I had forgotten about the presents. Those two never had their
presents ready to exchange on the festive occasion. They usually made them and, for some reason, made everyone else's
before they made each other's. Sometimes they were almost
a year late with a Christmas or birthday present. It got to be
a ritual. That silly card reminded me of Dani's horrible way
with words, but it also reminded me that Dani loved Dawn.
She did love Dawn Marie.

I have a picture in my head that is painful, one that I did
not mention as we sat around the pool and reminisced. When
Dani was about three years old, I decided that we needed to
do something special with each girl individually. Debra, first
born, would be the first to have a special event with her parents all to herself. We took her camping for the weekend.
We left Dani and Dawn home with Mrs. Frank, an elderly
lady from across the street. When we came home on Sunday
afternoon, Dani was sitting on the milkbox on the front porch.
She was all dressed up in a pretty little dress with crinolines

108

holding her skirt out like a tutu. And she was smiling that cheek-to-cheek smile that could tear your heart out. She had been sitting there all day, waiting for us; she was cold. I didn't realize that Mrs. Frank was just beginning to suffer the effects of Alzheimer's disease. She had dressed that child early in the morning and set her out there, telling her to look pretty so we would be glad to see her when we came home. And Dani bought it. She sat there all day in the chilly autumn air in her starched finery and waited to make us glad to see her. I still hurt when I remember that smile. I held my baby and loved her, but the hurt never went away. Mrs. Frank never babysat for us again, but nothing could give Dani back that day of waiting to be loved.

Very few people ever understood that Dawn and I could work together. It didn't look like we could. We yelled, we jostled, we bossed, we captured and recaptured the task, and we each appeared to doubt the abilities of the other. That is how it looked, but underneath all the noise and frustration was a deep conviction that there was no one else who could do this job as well as we could. I was in college at the same time Dawn was. I needed help with the graphics for my thesis. Dawn got a friend to drive her from Pullman to Spokane to deliver those graphics in time for my orals. They were exactly how I wanted them to be. We always knew exactly how the finished product should look and, without words, shared that view of the product. How we went about attaining it did cause a little friction, but our goal was always the same. We did a lot of volunteer work for the Symphony Society. Each year our family built and staffed a fair booth at the county fair. When the Whites left town, the symphony no longer had a fair booth. No one else gave a rap about county fairs, but we did so we designed and built and decorated a booth each year, incorporating the theme of the fair as best we could. Dawn and I were completely at ease with each other as we pushed and shoved and bossed each other around, but I did sometimes notice people around us studying us. When we moved to Bakersfield, we went to a Symphony Society fund-raiser fashion show. Dawn and I agreed that they needed us, that we could have done their graphics much better and could have organized their program better, too. They didn't get a chance to benefit from our expertise, but I am certain they would have loved the product and wondered at our method of working together. When we were together, we didn't think about how our behavior affected those around us. We concentrated so much on the task or the conversation that no one else really existed for us. There is no one left in this place that I trust enough to yell and boss and laugh too loud with while we work toward a common goal; there never was anyone else that understood that you could make that much noise and still trust each other completely and be delighted with the whole process.

Dawn Marie had a gas problem. She considered it her right and duty to get rid of that gas, refused to excuse herself, and required very slight acquaintance before subjecting one to her naturally occurring burps and farts. The burps were the worst. She ate; she burped—long and loud. Not a lot of burps, but one very, very loud, long burp. When she did it around me, it never failed to startle me and elicit a yelling match. "Da-a-a-awn! That is terrible! Excuse yourself! Nobody needs to burp like that. No wonder you aren't married. Who in this world would want to marry someone with a megaphone mouth like yours?"

And she invariably responded, "I *have* to burp when I eat. Do you want me to suffer?" And when she farted, she transferred that same megaphone to the other end. She had them all categorized; there were vegetable farts, bean farts, diet farts—all scientifically classified. I asked her how she got by at the office. I knew how she got by at school during those

110

all-nighter lab sessions: She burped and farted as if it were her right and her duty. Her friends sometimes commented/complained to me on the subject so I knew, but the office was different. There was a certain dignity and decorum to be maintained there. She said she saved it up and went into the bathroom. I said I pitied the next person to enter that bathroom. She then explained the air-exchange system to me and informed me that it was more than adequate to take care of any odor. Maybe it would be more factual to state that we had a problem with Dawn Marie's gas; she certainly didn't seem to consider it a problem.

Dawn was *funny*. She laughed just as loudly as she burped. She tolerated no phoniness or pretentiousness. She would allow no posturing, not even from her father. With his houseful of women, he always tried to maintain his modesty and reserve, especially when it came to women stuff. Dawn thought that was hilarious and would discuss her menstrual flow in front of her father. When he blushed, and he always blushed, she would grin from ear to ear and follow him around yelling, "Periods! Periods! Menstrua-a-a-ation!" He would invariable shout, "Dawn, that's terrible! Don't talk about that women stuff in front of me!" But she would not allow him to pretend that he was unaware of the details of menstruation and pregnancy. She was warm and good, and she almost made it to maturity.

Dani grew up almost without incident. She always tried to please and, like summer in some parts of Oregon, her teenage rebellion came on a weekend. She made arrangements to go to Portland to visit an old boyfriend. His mother had written to invite her, but Dani was afraid I wouldn't let her go so didn't tell me. I was, after all, the mother who made her give back the necklace. She told me she was going to visit a girl from our old neighborhood. Dawn went along to visit another girl from the same neighborhood. They rode the bus.

We were to meet their returning bus; they weren't on it. We went home and I began to search their room for clues. Somehow I knew they were in no danger, unless one were to consider my growing anger as dangerous. I found the letters from the boy and his mother. I called the girl's house where Dani was supposed to be staying. No, they hadn't seen her. I called the girl's house where Dawn was staying. Yes, they had left on time. Dawn had ridden the city bus to the downtown bus depot and waited there for Dani, who had extended her visit by a few hours. We met the next bus from Porland, at midnight. The girls were on it. We greeted them sweetly, loaded up their bags, and headed home. On the way, Pete asked Dani how her little girl friend was. Oh, she was fine. He waited. We got home. He asked her again. Same story. He confronted her. She told the truth. I put on my well-rehearsed and very dramatic scene, intended to put the fear of me and God, in that order, in the girls. We went to bed. That was the end of Dani's teenage rebellion, unless you count joining the navy when she was twenty-one, which she did count and I didn't.

Dawn, on the other hand, started her rebellion in the sixth grade and didn't stop until her junior year in college. My junior year in college brought a class that required that I write a term paper on a person I knew, diagnosing them according to the *Diagnostic and Statistical Manual*, third edition. I wrote about Dawn and made a pretty good case for a diagnosis of sociopathic personality disorder. She seemed to behave in a vacuum during those years, with no discernable remorse or consideration of the feelings of others. Because Dawn could read long before she started first grade, the teacher found several other students with Dawn's level of intelligence and the school district formed a special first grade for them. They were allowed to learn at their own pace, their questions were answered with more detail, and they were not particularly aware that they were more capable than their peers. This class continued for five years. During the sixth grade, the school principal retired; the new principal did not approve of that special class. He disbanded it and put those several students into a normal sixth grade with a first-year teacher whose former career had been driving a truck in Alaska. I began to hear rumors that all was not well in that classroom. Robbie Long, a neighbor boy, was transferred to another classroom; his mother said he was shaken and knocked against a locker by that new teacher. Dawn made clumsy attempts to tell me something was wrong, but I didn't hear her. Finally, I got a call from the new principal. Money was being stolen systematically from teachers' purses. They thought Dawn was involved. I did what any normal parent does: I denied that my daughter could possibly be involved. Adamantly.

Then a one-hundred–dollar bill was stolen from my purse. A couple of days later, Dani came and tearfully told me that Dawn had taken it. I lost any semblance of self-control, confronted Dawn, called the principal, and arranged for all the parents of all the students involved to meet with the principal and the teacher. We met in our family room. A hideous story came out of that meeting. The teacher had been unable to meet the challenge of these very bright youngsters. They finished any assigned work in minutes while other children took all week. He provided no other work for them to do and would allow them no freedom to work ahead or to work in greater depth. They were supposed to sit and wait. He did allow them trips to the library. On these trips, they foraged through empty classrooms and stole from teachers' purses. What did they do with the money? Tried to spend it all on candy, couldn't, and buried some of it in fields and orchards along the way to the store. We parents demanded that the classroom be investigated for violence, as the teacher had lost patience with the children and his own inability to handle them and manhandled them a bit. We then decided that all these six students must be suspended from school and not readmitted until parents could show that they had received counseling.

We took Dawn to a child psychiatrist who worked with our pediatrician. She went to a weekly session all summer long at fifty dollars per session. Pete and I waited in the lobby. Pete refused to go into the sessions, saying he hadn't stolen any money and wouldn't accept any punishment. At the end of the summer, the doctor found me in the lobby and invited me in for their last session. Dawn was mute. He told me that they had played hang-man and that, after he used the word *Czechoslovakia*, Dawn wouldn't play with him anymore, much less talk to him. And that was the way they had spent the summer, silently waiting for the hour to end: His assessment? Dawn was normal; the classroom had failed. Her assessment? He didn't play fair. How could he expect her to guess *Czechoslovakia*?

She went to public school the next year and was on the honor roll. The staff at the new school were more than able and willing to respond to her intelligence. They worked her and she loved it. She quit public school winners. I put all the girls in private school the next year. I was taking no more chances. There Dawn discovered just how poorly educated she was. We moved away at the end of that year. Looking back, I wish I had left the girls in that school as boarders. Maybe we could have prevented the entrance of that high school teacher into our lives. But probably not. Dawn's rebellion would have run its course. The cosmic dance would have been danced. If Only is not a good game to play, in life or in death.

Dawn matured very slowly, both physically and emotionally. She played with dolls long after her little sister stopped. Her best friend was six years younger than she. She had a complex Barbie housing development that she carefully maintained until she was sixteen years old, building new houses, sewing new clothes, and enacting new scenarios with those dolls. She began to menstruate when she was almost sixteen. It was Thanksgiving Day and all three generations were there, waiting for the turkey to come out of the oven. Dani came out of the bathroom and whispered to me that Dawn had started her first period. Word spread among the women in the kitchen and then leaked to the men in front of the fireplace. When Dawn came out of the bathroom and entered the dining room, she received a standing ovation from her smiling, nodding family. She was embarrassed, but she loved it.

Dawn eventually emerged intact from her troubled adolescent years. She never did develop morals that conformed to national standards, but in her way she was moral. During the required practicum for my degree in clinical psychology, I was assigned a family for counseling. They had been pushed into the mental health center by a son whose behavior confused and demoralized the parents. After just one or two sessions, I was able to tell them the story of Dawn's adolescence. This boy was the male counterpart of that girl; he was very, very bright, very eccentric, and unable to verbalize his discontent with some elements of their family life. Once we assured him that those elements would be worked on, he was excused to the lobby. I could assure those parents that he was fine, would be an admirable adult, but that it was never easy to raise these really bright ones. And then I rested; I was able at last to understand Dawn's adolescent years because I had been given an opportunity to look at it from the outside of a family, rather than from my entrenched position inside my own family. And Dawn was fine; she rested, too.

Dani almost starved when she moved into her new apartment after refusing to return to college. We worked together to furnish and decorate the apartment. I prepared and delivered a Care package of every staple I could grab as I whizzed down the aisles of a supermarket. Her cupboards were stocked.

115

She had a bed that looked like a couch during the day. She had a table made of a power company wire reel and wooden folding chairs. We bought a five-foot stepladder and set it up in the dining room to hold knickknacks and plants. Her collection of stuffed animals crowded every empty corner. There were framed family photographs and woven wall hangings. She was cozy and comfortable; I left and waved good-bye. She was just across town, but she was on her own. She wasn't encouraged to come over to visit too often, and her private life would now be just that—private. She began to budget her money to pay for rent, utilities, and phone and to buy food. She made a purchase that blew the budget; there was no recourse. She could not buy food. It was several months later that I learned that she had eaten pancakes made from the package of pancake flour in that reserve stock of staples for three weeks. She never did that again. After that incident, she taped several envelopes inside her cupboard door. Into each one went the portion of that check that was necessary to make the payment. Eventually, she graduated to a more abstract system of a checking account and journal. She never starved again and her credit was a matter of great pride.

Dawn learned from watching Dani. She had an allowance while away at college that had to stretch to cover dry cleaning, toiletries, entertainment, transportation, and any gift giving. She passed right over the envelope stage and went to a complex and very tidy journal in which she recorded every debt and every expenditure. Her attitude, however, was one of dire poverty. She could pull her face into the saddest, most dejected clown face and often did this face when discussing any purchase or possible expenditure. Even her eyes sagged. Dawn lived six years after she left home for college. She never stopped pulling that poor-mouth face whenever money was mentioned. She would become almost angry and declare loudly, "I can't afford that!" even when she could. From Sep-

116

tember until her death in February, I teased her about that face and her Depression attitude. I told her that the gods would hear her and she would be poor for the rest of her life. She did *not* see the humor in my teasing and did not change her attitude. She made almost every gift she gave us—such things as macramé wall hangings, paintings, drawings, a log-cabin—style pieced tea cozy, clothes. Those few items she bought are not treasured nearly as much, so I am grateful for her poor-mouth attitude when it was applied to gift giving. We all remember the way her features were pulled as if by an invisible string into a downward line—eyes, cheeks, mouth, chin, and head drooping—whenever someone suggested that she spend money she didn't have to spend for something she didn't have budgeted. Poor mouth!

For each of my daughters, at some time in their lives, I have had to pull out the stove in a grimy apartment and clean behind it. I did it for Debra when she divorced her first husband and moved into a low-rent first-floor portion of an old house in Boise, Idaho. The apartment had been the living room, dining room, and den of a once elegant home. It was filthy and in bad repair. Dawn, Darcy, and I drove the five hours from the Tri-Cities to Boise; we arrived just after noon. We sat in the apartment for twenty minutes, sizing it up, and then we descended on a paint store. I cleaned while Dawn and Darcy painted. When the cleaning was done, I painted with Darcy while Dawn wallpapered. We even painted the ceilings, the fireplace, and the outside of the bathtub. We painted all night, finally collapsing across Debra's bed as the sun was just peeking over the mountains to the east. The stove and refrigerator were stuck to the floor in a collection of grime of Smithsonian quality. I pulled them out and soaked the floor with straight bleach and then crawled in it to scrape the ancient linoleum as clean as it would come. When Dani moved off the base to a house in a subdivision, I flew to Florida to

117

jerk the stove and fridge loose from another pile of grease and debris. We didn't have to paint that house, but we did wash down every surface and shampoo the carpets into the wee small hours of the morning.

Dawn lived in the dorm for her freshman and sophomore years. She moved to a second-floor apartment carved out of an old house near campus at the beginning of her junior year. I didn't see the apartment for several months; Dawn had built a cabinet and painted the living room and kitchen before I got there. That summer she moved out of the apartment, reserving it for the next fall term, so that she wouldn't have to pay rent during the summer. She moved back in the next fall without my help. The next summer, overriding her poor-mouth objections, we talked her into paying rent through the summer, thereby eliminating the move into storage of her furnishings and clothes. She and I drove to Pullman in early September to open the apartment and get her settled for the school year. We were to clean and then we would paint her bedroom and her dresser. A good friend of hers was moving into the upstairs apartment while we worked. He came down to inform us that they had pulled out the stove and were absolutely amazed at what they found under it. I looked at Dawn. She looked at me and said, "I tried to pull mine out but it is bolted to the floor." I didn't answer. The conversation with her friend went on. I went back to removing the mold from the refrigerator they had unplugged and left with the door closed. It hit me. Bolted to the floor? Who ever bolted a stove to a floor? I called her from the bedroom. We tugged, we pried, we jerked, we pushed, we pulled, and the stove broke loose. Then we got the fridge loose. And we bleached, we scoured, we scooped, we gagged, we choked, we scrubbed; we returned both appliances to an absolutely pristine corner of the kitchen.

Then we painted the ceiling. We had no ladder. We had

118

one chair and the dresser. We moved the dresser around the room, balanced on its shaky top, and painted the twelve-foot ceiling. When going got really rough, we put the chair on top of the dresser and painted. We were completely content, yelling at each other, criticizing each other's work, grabbing tools from each other, in our drive to complete the task exactly as we thought it should be. Then we scraped the worst of the splattered paint off of the dresser and painted it, too.

Probably as a hangover from Dawn's horrible adolescence, I never learned to trust her driving. It was my last bastion of distrust when the adolescence was over and Dawn was a grown woman. She drove home from Pullman that night. We were exhausted. It was late. I fell asleep, but jerked awake every few miles to demand to know how fast she was going and to accuse her of throwing me around the car with her wild, unskilled cornering. She reassured me each time, never losing patience with my quite unconcealed distrust of her skill.

Dawn trusted no one's driving, least of all Dani's—which was strange, because Dani was probably the best driver in the family. We went to Disneyland one weekend between Thanksgiving and Christmas. Dani drove my car; Dawn, Darcy, and I were passengers. Going down was uneventful. Dawn may have slept. Coming home was quite another matter. We had to drive the Grapevine, a very dangerous stretch of highway between Los Angeles and Bakersfield with a long, steep downgrade. Trucks often have brake failures there; people are killed there with a distressing regularity. The trucks are supposed to stay in the outside two lanes; cars should stay in the inside lanes. Dawn was convinced that the farthest inside lane was for high speel travel only. As we drove home in the afternoon and evening twilight, Dawn's long body uncurled itself many times to lean across the back of the seat so she could yell at Dani that she must not drive in this inside lane if she was not going to go faster. She could not be convinced that the speed limit was really fast enough. Having just come from Disneyland, we were freshly reminded that Dawn hated the "It's a Small World" exhibit. Dawn never disliked anything—she *hated* it! And she hated "It's a Small World." As we became more exasperated with her diatribe from the back seat about the required speed for driving in the inside lane, we winked at each other and started to sing, "It's a small world after all. It's a small world after all." She leaned back against the seat, crossed her arms over her chest, and sulked. She couldn't maintain the sulk, nor could she remain silent about the speed in the inside lane. Every time she leaned forward, we sang; every time we sang, she leaned back. We did that all the way home.

Dani spoiled all animals, but she preferred dogs to cats. Dawn didn't spoil anything or anybody, but she preferred cats to dogs. Dani was quickly trained by our little black poodle, Mortimer, to give back rubs. He would jump into her lap, turn his back to her, and wait. She would give him a massage from tail to shoulders that would have been the envy of any massage parlor patron. I kept telling her that she was spoiling him for everyone else, because all of his endearing little tricks had been reduced to that one black back in one's face, begging to be massaged. Dawn didn't massage Mort. She wasn't even very nice to him. He seemed to like her even though she played basketball head with him. He has a Dutch clip that makes the top of his head look round. She would place her palm on his head and bounce his head up and down, while chanting, "Basketball head. Basketball head." Mort put up with being dribbled; if it was all he could get from her, he would take it.

Dawn bought herself a cat. Peepers was the scroungiest-looking cat I ever saw. Skinny, whiney, restless—a lot like the young Dawn, come to think of it. She loved Peepers, but

120

no one else in this world would or did. She did not spoil him, however. He wanted to sleep with her. She let him start the night there, but the slightest sound or relocation of position would cause him to find himself on the other side of a closed door. Peepers was not one to take this lightly. He would scratch at the door, meow loudly, and stalk up and down the hall. And Dawn didn't take that lightly. Their nights together were marked by recurrent guerrilla warfare. Dawn wouldn't let Peepers go outside and she was too cheap to buy as much litter as it took for that greedy cat to live indoors all the time. Her room stunk! Poor Peepers had to sort through old poop to find a place to deposit new poop. But no one could tell Dawn anything. She would buy more kitty litter when it was budgeted and not before. She would let poor old Peepers outdoors when she trusted him to stay nearby and not before. Peepers went to live with Paul, Dawn's friend from work, when Dawn died. Paul says Peepers has developed into a perfectly normal cat, now that he can get a good night's sleep and go potty outdoors or in a clean litter box.

There were so many ways in which Dawn and Dani were similar and, at the same time, different from the other children. They had nicknames. No one else did. Dani was Lynn Dan Johnson; in the next breath, she might be Dan'l Boone Bear. Dawn was Dawn Marezie, Dawn Burezie, Breezie, and Dawnzie. The names were interchangeable and used all the time. When Dawn was about twelve, she called a family council meeting. She didn't like her name. (I *loved* that name!) She wanted to be called something else.

"Well, that's pretty normal. Lots of people don't like their names and want to be called something different. What do you want to be called?" her father queried.

"Marie."

"Marie? Okay, we will make a real effort to remember to call you Marie." He even bought her a name tag, which

121

she wore for a week or two, until she got tired of being Marie. She never got tired of being Breezie.

The one characteristic of the girls we all remember as being very different from the rest of us was their approach to machinery. Both of them read the instruction book *before* they took the machine out of the case. By the time they had the machine in operation, be it sewing machine, calculator, car, motorcycle, hairdryer, or whatever, they knew everything that machine would do and how to make it do it. Dawn had a stereo system that I now have in my family room. I sort of hope she doesn't know I have it; I was never allowed to touch it when she was alive. If I walked toward it with the intention of changing a tape or a record, she would look intensely at me and walk between me and the machine. She would challenge me as if I were on forbidden territory, like a federal reserve or something. "What do you want? I'll do it." And then she would continue to stare at me as if to wordlessly inquire what in the world I thought I was doing even *thinking* about touching that machine.

I drove Dani's car once. We were on a trip to North Carolina from Florida on the back roads, seeing villages and countryside. We were supposed to take turns driving. Well, I left the emergency brake a little bit on. Such disgust. She almost cried. She told me I had ruined the trade-in value of the car. She glared at me. She withdrew into hostile silence. I tried to reassure her that the brake had not gotten hot, we hadn't smelled anything, it was only a little bit on, nothing had happened. She did not believe me; she did believe that I had ruined the brakes. She worked it out so that I didn't drive any more on that trip. Both of the girls believe that they were the only people in the world who knew how to treat their machines, but when the machines did malfunction, they did not believe that anyone in the world could fix them. They were devastated! They were without hope! They were depressed! They were sad! They were insulted! Pete and I would reassure them and call a repairman for them, but they never trusted a machine that had failed them, not ever again.

Our mourning wasn't just reminiscing in the sun. If we had been watched closely, we could easily have been judged insane. We did crazy things—and one should! I went into the guest room each morning and said good morning to the girls' pictures. Dawn's college graduation picture that she spent her own money on especially for me is hanging over one bed. Dani's Sailor of the Month picture is hanging over the other. The walls of the room are crowded with framed photos from every school year and every memorable event. I stood there each morning and looked into the girls' laughing eyes and talked to them. One day, Dawn stopped being a face in a photograph and became living, breathing flesh while I watched. Tears streamed down my face while I thanked her for smiling at me from a living face. For months, that photograph came alive for me whenever I studied it for any length of time. Some days I cried all day long. I sobbed while I washed dishes, while I weeded flower beds, while I made the beds. I talked to the girls. When I broke something of theirs, I apologized. No one heard me or saw me do these things, and I am glad they didn't. But they needed to be done. And I did them.

Chapter Eight

When the girls died, people said to us, "Oh, what a terrible tragedy." I invariably replied, "I don't know the dictionary definition of a tragedy, but I don't feel like this is one." I think I reacted that way because I didn't like being perceived as a loser. We have always been winners; we don't always win, but we are winners. That these deaths could happen in our family put us in a losing position. And losers are vulnerable. There were people who responded to that supposed vulnerability. People who, years before, had been eliminated from our circle of friends and family life because of undesirable behavior decided to come to the funeral. I wondered why. They didn't know the girls, not having seen them since infancy and never having shared any of their life experiences. They weren't our friends, partly because they had never exhibited any sensitivity or caring. So what prompted them to want to join us in the celebration of the lives of our girls?

I think they wanted to come for two reasons. The first: they wanted to watch us suffer. We had rejected them and now they could watch us react when the gods had finally gotten us. They could neither celebrate nor mourn the girls, but they could gloat when we were down. The second possible reason for their desire to be there was their perception of an opportunity to walk back into our lives with all previous commissions and omissions forgotten in the turmoil of emotions surrounding the deaths. Vultures and jackals coming out of the bush after the kill, they telephoned from the distant past and invited themselves to the funeral. They were refused, spurned, turned back into the bush. There is a vulture and a jackal in each of us; I needed to defend against that element in myself and in others when I made that funeral a celebration of life. There would be nothing in that ceremony or in our behavior that would intimate that the gods had gotten us. Our grief would be private; our joy would be public. The voyeurs would have to go away disappointed.

But was it a tragedy? The dictionary says yes. A tragedy is "an intensely sad, calamitous, or fatal event." This event was fatal; therefore, it was tragic. Darcy told me the other day that Arthur Miller said, in reference to *Death of a Salesman*, that a tragedy was that circumstance in which there was a specific point at which one could choose other actions and consequences. I like that. There was no point in Dani and Dawn's lives at which one could say, "This specific behavior was wrong; this choice could have been made differently with less calamitous results." In the billions of milliseconds of their lives, each behavior and each choice led quietly and directly to that spot at the curve in the road, and the approaching big car with the little driver was not part of a tragedy, according to Arthur Miller. But lurking in the dark regions of my mind are the Greek dramas in which a person of greatness is struck down because of some flaw in his character. Somehow I need to defend against the nasal screech of the ancient hags residing in the primitive regions of my brain; I need to tell them that my daughters did not die because of some flaw in their character nor was it a flaw in our character that caused us to suffer their loss.

The yogis say that when a young person dies, they are merely changing locations in order to have a better opportunity to work out their karma; they have done what they can here and must move on in order to continue to develop. They say there is simply a relocation from this life, through death, to another life. Life is a place for learning and growing; when one has exhausted those possibilities here, one moves on to a higher school. The school is for removing flaws in our character, the karma that must be worked out by learning and growth. So, hush, you old crones. The yogis are right; so is Arthur Miller.

People write letters and make phone calls and, in the face of their own discomfort and ignorance, say, "It's hard to know why God does these things." My dear friend George Ball wrote: "There must be something in the mind of God that would bring resolution and peace but it is beyond me." The peace and resolution come from knowing that death and life are not in the mind of God; they are in the mind of man. When a caterpillar winds himself into his cocoon and emerges a butterfly, we celebrate the emergence of the butterfly. But what if you were another caterpillar? All you see is the loss of your friend and the empty cocoon where a life you shared used to be. Do you suppose that caterpillars stomp around and shake their legs in God's face and say, "How can you allow this to happen to me? How can you take away my friend?" What tolerance God must have, to smile and say, "Silly caterpillar, don't display your ignorance quite so noisily. It all depends on your point of view."

Point of view. That is what we are to God: His point of viewing this reality. He created it and was too big to play in it, so made us to experience it for him. Did you ever build a playhouse or a sand castle or a tiny boat so perfect and enchanting that you wished yourself inside it to experience life in your miniature creation? Did you ever sit with your eye to the window of a model house or boat and imagine yourself able to walk through the tiny halls and sit in the tiny chairs? If you were God and you built a universe like this one, you would be too big to play here; the difference is that God can wish creation. He wished us to experience this little toy universe for him. And when a child moves little dolls around a model house, the doll is often snatched out of the house to be redressed or moved to another position in the imagined story being enacted there. The other dolls would be out of line to stomp and growl and whine because their associate had been moved. How silly. It is only a story being acted out, only a pretend visit to a tiny creation, so the dolls shouldn't take it seriously, but should wait to see what new dress and what new role and what new room the child outside the miniature window has planned for their friend. The child knows the doll continues to exist and will soon be back in the story. The doll that is being redressed knows it, too. Only the dolls left in the doll house have such a limited point of view that they may worry about being left. So it all depends on your point of view, and in God's point of view, there is no life and there is no death. There is only a play in a tiny little universe.

So how should one mourn, since mourn we must? I am so glad you asked; there are many instructions I want to give; there is so much hard-learned knowledge to share now that I have returned from the borders of the place. I discovered that there is an underground, secret society of ex-mourners who know these things but don't dare tell you because they feel you will think they are ghoulish or just plain nuts—and there are mourners who refused to mourn so must continue to suffer and never know the joy and wonder of the lands near the border. Mourning is a task that must be done and one can take great pride in having done it well, so when it comes your time to mourn, approach it as a fascinating new experience and stay open to whatever experiences come.

Take one step back from your mourning. Do it, but *watch*

yourself doing it. Do whatever feels right and good, whatever your cultural or religious background provides for you in the way of ceremony and community, but maintain a point of view somewhat removed from the mourning and the ceremony. Somehow that one-step–removed position takes you one step closer to God and one step further from ignorance and pain.

Go ahead and hurt. Pain and growth are inseparable, if one will allow oneself to feel the pain. Don't accept the pity and the pills and the dull, gray fog of denial and withdrawal. Get in there and explore the territory. There is growth here and great joy in shared sympathy and love. Welcome the growth and accept the pain that accompanies it.

Know that the first few days are a time of shock and numbness and know that the numbness will wear off, just about when everybody goes home and leaves you alone. When the pain becomes overwhelming, tell God and demand the comfort He promises in almost every culture and religion. Just scream, "Hey, God! This play is not fun or funny. You are writing the script. You cast me in this role. I need better direction. Help me!" He will; He does. And that help is one of the wonders of the place called Death.

Know that anger follows the pain if you are not prepared for it. You can forestall it and you should because it is destructive and what gets destroyed is you. Remember what the yogi told Pete and me? "Smile and send love." That advice is foolproof. If you begin your mourning by sending love, you cannot become angry with that person. Before you are ready for anger, you have established the habit of smiling when you think of him or her and of loving that one intensely whenever you think of them. The yogi said that they will know you are loving them and will benefit from it; I know that you will benefit from forestalling anger with love and smiles.

Know that you will be a little bit crazy while you mourn.

Fortunately, you will not remember everything you did or said; if you have good friends, they will never remind you. Allow yourself to be a little crazy; don't hold yourself to any rigid standards of behavior. What you feel is right for you is probably fine with everyone around you, and if not, they will forgive you if it doesn't last too long. The only thing you cannot forgive yourself is the lack of the courage to mourn. Your energy levels will be lower; you will catch every bug that comes around. Your decisions may not be as sound as they seem at the time, so don't sell the house or make any momentous choices. What you do with the *things* is not momentous. One of the lessons of mourning is the unimportance of what happened to the underwear and sweaters and suits and possessions of the deceased. You may find that your whole attitude toward possessions is greatly altered. I was delighted to discover that I no longer needed the careful list attached to my will. I don't give a rap who gets the silver; I won't be around to know about it, anyway.

Treat yourself as if you had just had major surgery. You have had a major part of your life removed and it does weaken you for a while. Widow's weeds and black armbands are no longer in fashion in our culture. One is expected to jump right back into life as if nothing has happened, but something has happened. You are in a major growth phase and operating at different energy levels than those around you. Take your time and take it easy.

If your particular community is one in which denial of the death is demanded, rebel. Bury your own dead, if you can. Do not play the game that there is no corpse, there is no dirt, there is no hole in the ground three feet wide and six feet long. Just as an expectant mother no longer goes to a hospital delivery room expecting to be anesthetized, so the mourners should no longer expect to have the details of the death hidden from them. Dress your dead and walk with them to their grave and bury them. It is much more difficult for the furies to lie to you when you have seen the evidence and buried your own dead.

Above all, be willing to mourn and be willing to cease mourning.

I had a dream the other night. I answered the phone and it was Dawn calling me from Heaven. We talked for a minute and then we were cut off. I woke with a start and whispered a prayer that we could be reconnected. I snuggled back into sleep so I would be ready for the return call. It came. She talked and talked, just as she always did. I was delighted that I could recall her voice so perfectly, because even as I listened to her ramble on, I was aware that I was the dreamer and therefore the creator of this voice in my ear. Dawn's voice was a machine-gun monotone. She had almost no inflection in her voice, but she talked *fast*. When she was sleepy or tired or depressed, she slowed down; when she was excited, she sped up. When she was really excited, she was unintelligible. Her friend Michael used to snort and exclaim, "Oh, that voice! She could talk for hours and never change her inflection." The only deviation from her one-note was the imitation of sounds. Dani imitated people; Dawn imitated machines and sounds produced by people. Most things made the sound "Geesh." Chairs sounded like that when they turned; brakes made that sound; anything dropped or thrown made that sound as it went through the air. She didn't imitate any sounds while we talked on the phone in my dream. She just talked in her machine-gun monotone, relating how busy she was and all the activities she was involved in. As in life, I did not pay much attention to the content; I just enjoyed the contact.

Dawn has come to visit me twice since she died and she has called me once. Why not Dani? I was closer to Dani in life. Dawn was Pete's favorite; Dani was mine. I think about that. Dani's helpful presence was obvious to me just after they

130

died, but it soon faded. Dawn didn't leave so soon, and when she did leave, she still came around to call. Why? I think Dani didn't need to finish any business with me. We were friends with everything said; there was no unfinished business. And she had Roy. They were together. They were more adult, had given more thought to life after death and were better prepared to make a quick adjustment to their new circumstances. Dawn was not quite finished growing up and did not consider herself to be mortal. She was angry at finding herself dead; she had things that needed to be said and done here; she wasn't ready to look around and scout out her new territory. So, as she did in life, she came home to just be there and talk, saying nothing of any importance, loving with her presence and her rambling conversation.

Sometimes Pete and I sat together in the car or by the winter fire and Pete would say to me, "I miss those girls. Sometimes I miss them so much." We do. We miss them. But that doesn't mean we still mourn them. We miss them as if they have gone to darkest Africa for the Peace Corps or are on a wonderful tour of the Continent for a long period of time. We are happy they are where they are, but we are selfish enough to miss them while they are not here.

My clinical advisor and thesis advisor in grad school became my good friend. We worked together the year after I graduated, establishing an off-campus campus for the clinical psychology program. Bob also acted as director of outpatient services at the mental health center where I was director of support services. I have great respect for his abilities; more than that, he is my friend. In October, I returned with Pete to the Tri-Cities. Pete had business meetings and I wanted to visit with my old friends. Bob and I met for lunch. We talked about the mourning process; he is, after all, a psychologist with a doctoral degree, and I was getting his services for free. I called him immediately after the girls died. He listened;

131

he does that very well. After a quiet pause, he said, "Well, you certainly have a piece of me." I used that piece frequently at first and then less and less often. This lunch was the occasion for returning that piece of him to its owner. Tears flowed freely while I talked, but I was not really crying, just dripping tears. I told him that, although only six months had passed and everyone knows that it takes a year to finish mourning, I thought I had completed my task. I really couldn't see anything more for me to do. He thought about it for a moment and then instructed me, "I think you have finished 80 or 90 percent of the task and the other 10 or 20 percent is never finished." Yes. He is right. We tried to think of the right word to describe that part of me that is what is left of the girls. We thought of *dregs* and discarded it. *Residue*. That is the word. There is a residue of what they were that has become part of what I am.

On February 24, 1985, the whole family went to the cemetery. We took bouquets of wildflowers, scrub brushes to clean the headstones, a crowbar to lift the vases from inside the markers, and a camera. We cut back the grass and polished the stones. We sat in the sun and looked out over the valley. We took photographs of the family sitting between the two graves. There was absolutely no sense that the girls were there or that they were aware of what we were doing; they were only aware of the love that inspired this little ceremony. Our little grandson walked away from us to an unfinished part of the cemetery where there were large round stones exposed in the dirt. One by one, he carried rocks to a place between the two headstones, sweating and trudging back and forth across the hillside. Each rock was placed carefully on top of the one before it. He built a cairn. We watched, awed by the intuitive understanding of death displayed by this little guy, not quite three years old. When the cairn was of satisfactory size, he rested and wiped perspiration from his brow. I wrote to my friend Rhoda and told her what he had done. She replied: "Edward has wisdom."

On the way home, Darcy told me of the dream she had dreamed repeatedly during the early part of the last year. She was riding in the car with Roy and Dani and Dawn. The car came around the corner and hit their car, killing everyone but her. She witnessed the blood and the mangled bodies and the quiet after the explosive crash and wondered and agonized that she was still alive while they were dead. I asked her if she understood why she had that dream. She responded that she did, that she, too, had met the furies and their ancient anger that somehow she had allowed death and sorrow to penetrate their kingdom. She understood that this was guilt, but not a real guilt; she, too, had quieted the furies.

The year is over. I had forgotten how much energy I normally have. I had forgotten that I giggle and wise-crack and clown. I thought I was behaving normally during that year, but now that I am myself again, I realize how different I was while I mourned. But I am better for having mourned. I am richer, drawn in more intense colors. I am wiser for having walked with the girls through the valley of the shadow of death, the place with the wide boundaries, roped off with gossamer curtains of light. I left them there, at the entrance. They have gone on to experience fully the land of thought forms and color and light. I have returned to this quiet, slow, heavy existence. I have quilted the quilts they left unfinished. I have completed the scrapbooks; the end of their lives is also chronicled.

And I am intensely aware that the girls have not, and will not ever really be gone from my life. Somehow, they are more present than they were when they lived. They don't change; they don't bring home problems; they don't move away and neglect to write; they don't argue with me; they remain constant. Deep inside my being, they smile. I am a repository of their smiles.

My friend Lorie sent me the epitaph from a mass grave for Vietnamese orphans, which reads: "Those who love you will behold you across ten thousand worlds of birth and death." Yes. I gaze lovingly toward that world and know that they are looking back at us. Not longingly, but lovingly, we behold each other across infinite places of life and death. Life and death are separate places, but the borders are transparent and interpenetrating.